THROUGH THE

VALLEY

Mikayla's Story

Laura Gyfteas

"Yea, though I walk through the valley of the shadow of death, I will fear no evil: for thou art with me; thy rod and thy staff they comfort me."

Psalm 23:4

Copyright © 2011 by Laura Gyfteas

All rights reserved. No portion of this book may be reproduced, stored in a retrieval system, or transmitted in any form or by any means-electronic, mechanical, recordings, scanning, or other- except for brief quotations in printed reviews, without the prior written permission of the author.

Requests for permission should be addressed to:
Laura Gyfteas
C/O Abracadabra
P.O. Box 102062
Anchorage, Alaska 99510

All scripture quotations are taken from the Holy Bible, *King James Version*.

AUTHOR'S NOTE: Characters and circumstances in this book are real and true, described from the author's memory of events.

Gyfteas, Laura
> *Through The Valley: Mikayla's Story*

ISBN-13: 978-1463781675
ISBN-10: 1463781679

For Mikayla, Taki, and Akylas,
our three precious miracles,

And for our family and friends, who stayed by
our side to help us go through the valley.
We are forever grateful for your unending love and
support.

Most scriptures referenced within this story were
shared with me by family and friends as a means of
encouragement to lift our spirits during such a time,
and to remind us of the promises and hope God has
given his children. Thank you, dear family and friends,
for your thoughts, words, and reminders of God's
truths.

INTRODUCTION

"Come unto me, all ye that labour and are heavy laden, and I will give you rest."
~Matthew 11:28

This story, though brief and containing a happy ending, is the substance of every parent's worst nightmare – walking with your own child through a life-threatening illness, knowing that in the end, the illness could very well win the battle. These types of internal medical struggles can take days, weeks, months, or even years. We enter the fight knowing we could lose everything in the end. The very nature of our bodies can prove their own fragility as they go down in the arduous fight.

Or we can win.

Unfortunately, whether we will win or lose is

unpredictable; but still, we fight. We pour everything we have into that battle.

Cancer is like that for me, and it is one of my greatest fears since I became a parent. It is an unknown entity, cruel in the way it can overcome its victims…but, it is also *not* a certain victor. Not every time.

Countless funds have been given to medical research as humans struggle to gain the upper hand over this random attack on the lives of so many. Slowly but surely, advances are made. New treatments are found. Cancer *can* be beaten after all. It will not always conquer.

I have proof of that fact every time I look in my daughter's eyes – bright, vibrant, and glowing with life and vitality.

I have previously said, "I can't imagine having to go through cancer with one of my children. I don't know how I could bear it."

And then suddenly – causing me to remember my words and cringe – there it was. Cancer. Like a natural disaster disrupting our predictably safe lives, that life-threatening word abruptly entered my world. I could perhaps compare it to something as shattering as an earthquake or tornado; it was that unexpected and unbelievable. Our particular natural disaster came in the form of one of the many different types of cancer, in my perfect little girl, Mikayla, who was only three years old.

But bear it we did – what choice was there? The battle had commenced in my own home, in the body of one of those most precious to me.

Here is the story of our journey together, step by step and day by day.

CHAPTER ONE

~ The Beginning ~

"God is our refuge and strength, a very present help in trouble."
~Psalm 46:1

In November of 2004, we welcomed our firstborn, a beautiful and perfect baby daughter, Mikayla. From the very beginning, we called her our precious little miracle. And that is what she is. God created her, breathed life into her tiny body, and presented us with an amazing gift on that wonderful day.

My husband, Kosta, and I were in awe of her. Ten perfect fingers; ten little toes. An adorable nose and velvety cap of dark hair. Half of our friends said she looked just like her daddy, while just as many people thought the resemblance was mostly to me.

She grew to be a beautiful toddler who was both reserved and intelligent.

Almost four years later, we entered the hardest phase of our entire lives. With children – Mikayla and her nineteen-months-younger brother, Taki – we had already been through the usual small trials such as colds, ear infections, or bumps and bruises from everyday play. But nothing – *nothing* – could have prepared us for what we experienced next. On October 21, 2008, a large tumor was found in our precious little girl.

It began with a kidney infection on June 8, 2008. Mikayla seemed fine that day. There was no great symptom manifesting, or a feeling of uneasiness to warn us of what might come in the following months. Her little brother had celebrated his birthday on the day before. We attended a housewarming party and Mikayla ran around the yard there for over an hour, playing with her friends. We went home and Mikayla climbed into her bed for a nap. It was all perfectly normal, as most of our days are.

Less than an hour later, Mikayla woke up crying and said her tummy hurt, and that she needed to throw up. I gave her children's Pepto Bismol, hoping it was just an upset tummy from something she ate and not a flu bug. However, half an hour later, she was crying again. Then the symptoms set in. For the next hour she laid on the bathroom floor with me sitting next to her. She alternated between extreme lethargy, almost sleeping, and then several minutes of moaning that her tummy hurt. She had very little strength.

Since this was not a normal stomachache, I thought it could be her appendix and called my mom, a nurse, who drove to our house right away. She looked up the symptoms online and they matched appendicitis, so I called my husband at work and told him I was preparing to take Mikayla in to the Emergency Room at the hospital nearby.

I had never taken either of our children to the emergency room before, and packed for the trip in a state of nervous apprehension. I put several floppy books, Mikayla's blankie, favorite bear MoMo, and a change of clothes in her backpack. I carefully outfitted her in a simple pull-on dress so she would be more comfortable when doctors had to start examining her. Poking around Mikayla's abdomen would be painful enough. I didn't want to make it harder by having cumbersome clothing in the way. Getting her in the car seat was a lot of work, and she cried out in pain several times.

The car trip was difficult. I always thought our roads were easy to navigate, but this trip felt anything but smooth. Even the smallest bump made Mikayla whimper, and my heart broke to see her in pain. I glanced at her in the rearview mirror repeatedly, and prayed that the stoplights would all be green.

My dad and his wife met us at the hospital. I sat in the waiting room for about half an hour, holding Mikayla as she slumped against me. She was sleeping off and on, waking only to fidget and moan of the pain in her tummy. By this time, I was imagining surgery and was teary-eyed and tired. My dad and stepmom comforted me as I waited for Kosta to arrive. Mikayla vomited her lunch as we waited, although fortunately, she was old enough to give us a warning. My dad immediately jumped up and grabbed the nearest trash can, saving us the trouble of cleaning up a mess.

Kosta arrived as we were being shown to an examining room, and I felt like I had never been so happy to see him. We did our best to entertain Mikayla, reading through several of the books we had brought and pausing frequently to comfort her as she cried from either the pain or being scared. Nurses came in and out, a doctor examined her, and tests were run.

Four tense hours later, Mikayla was diagnosed with a kidney infection, which can have many of the same symptoms as appendicitis. She was given a shot of antibiotics, which was by far the most traumatizing part of the whole experience for her. The approaching needle terrified her and she did not want to relinquish her leg, but finally, it was over. Though concerned about the infection, I was also vastly relieved that she did not have appendicitis, which would have required surgery. I just couldn't imagine my three-year-old having an operation.

That night, Mikayla slept next to me. Appendicitis had not yet been ruled out completely, and I needed to keep watch over her in case she got worse. Thankfully, she slept well, exhausted from her ordeal. For two days she was lethargic, had no strength or energy, and spent much of her time on the couch. She continued antibiotics for ten days and we went to our family doctor to follow up. The kidney infection had stemmed from a urinary tract infection (UTI) that had been untreated. At her age, this can be easily missed by a parent as very young children often do not have the pain associated with urination that older children and adults experience.

Mikayla took a urine test at the hospital and another at our doctor's office for the follow-up. Sadly, she became familiar with going potty in a cup.

The infection was still present, so round two of the antibiotics began. At the end of the second antibiotic, she took another urinalysis and the infection was still there, but our doctor did not want her continuing more antibiotics. Instead, she drank cranberry juice all week in an attempt to rid her body of the last vestiges of infection. It finally went away completely nearly a month after the trip to the hospital.

Our doctor told us that Mikayla might be prone to more infections and if she had another one soon, she could be referred to an urologist to see if there was a vesicoureteral reflux. She explained that urine flows downward from the kidneys to the ureters and then to the bladder. This particular reflux is the abnormal flow from the bladder back up into the ureters, which can lead to a urinary tract infection. If Mikayla had another infection, a specialist would determine if further testing should be done to see if the reflux was present. Kosta and I were relieved that the infection had finally gone, and hoped that would be the end of it.

Unfortunately, three months later, another urinary tract infection appeared. In late September, Mikayla woke up crying in the middle of the night and said it hurt when she went potty. We took her to our doctor, who confirmed the presence of another UTI and Mikayla began antibiotics again. Our doctor referred her to an urologist to be certain that these infections were not related to a greater problem. When round one of antibiotics finished, Mikayla still had the infection and we started her on a different antibiotic, hoping the alternate medicine would work better. In early October, I took Mikayla to the pediatric urologist.

The visit began easily enough with a urinalysis. However, when the nurse wheeled in a small ultrasound machine on a cart, Mikayla started crying. She was scared of the strange new machine and thought it meant she would get a shot. With her hands over her mouth and tears pouring down her cheeks, she looked at me and cried, "I don't want to get a shot!"

It took me several minutes to calm Mikayla down and assure her that an ultrasound would not hurt at all. I finally used the analogy of the machine being a camera that could take a picture of the inside of Mikayla's tummy, telling her that my camera wasn't good enough to take a picture like that. She calmed down considerably. When they began the ultrasound and it did not hurt at all, she relaxed a bit more, although she clung to me and remained tense throughout the procedure.

The urologist examined her briefly and said that there was a possibility she had a vesicoureteral reflux. He referred us to the hospital for a renal kidney ultrasound, which would be painless. He also required Mikayla to undergo a voiding cystourethrogram, a procedure that examines the flow to and from the bladder by using a liquid that can be seen on an imaging screen and is placed through a catheter. He prescribed a sedative to help Mikayla relax for this procedure and not have pain during the catheter insertion.

Mikayla finished the antibiotics and I was nervous that she would be off the medication for nine days before the procedures would take place. I did not want a repeat of the kidney infection, as we learned that kidneys can be damaged through severe or multiple infections. Even though I was not looking forward to my daughter needing these procedures, I hoped to get them done as soon as possible so we could resolve any problems.

On the Saturday before the scheduled hospital trip, Mikayla contracted stomach flu. She vomited twice and I wondered if this related to the kidneys, since she'd experienced vomiting previously when she had a kidney infection. However, my son vomited the following morning so we knew that it was the flu and Mikayla's kidneys were fine so far. She recovered quickly, though she was still not back to eating normally three days later when the procedures began.

October 21, 2008

Tuesday morning did not start out as planned. I put Mikayla to bed late the night before, hoping that she would sleep in and wake up just before we needed to give her the sedative, as she had to fast for the ultrasound. She was a light eater anyway and hopefully wouldn't have much time to realize that she was hungry. Instead, she woke up two hours early. She had eaten very little during the prior day because of the flu and was hungry, so we tried to explain to her that she was required to have an empty stomach and full bladder.

How do you explain such a thing to a three-year-old? Yes, it's breakfast time, but no, you can't have anything. Poor Mikayla.

Instead, we diverted her attention away from hunger by putting on a movie, and she happily watched *Care Bears* for the next hour. I could only give her clear liquids and she wasn't drinking as much water as she needed to fill her bladder, so I gave her some fruit juice as well. I had reservations about that, considering it was a lot of sugar for an empty and just-been-sick tummy, but what else could we do? The doctor had been clear that the bladder had to be full.

Just before noon, we gave her the first sedative. The doctor had given us two doses in case the first did not calm Mikayla enough. We got the kids in the car and started driving to a friend's house to drop off our son. Unfortunately, Mikayla was having diarrhea all morning. I didn't know if it was related to flu, nervousness about the hospital visit, or a combination of both, but every few minutes she started crying because she needed to go again. I was hoping that she wouldn't go potty at the same time because she'd drunk barely enough to fill her bladder for the ultrasound!

A half-hour after the first sedative dose, she became groggy but was still extremely nervous, so I gave her the second dose. The procedure was to occur at 12:45 p.m., about a half-hour after the second dose. After two doses, I was sure Mikayla would be relaxed enough for the procedure.

After our son was dropped off and we were driving to the hospital, Mikayla looked out her window toward the heavens. There was nothing there except tree tops and a clear sky, but the sedative apparently made her see more.

"Mommy…there's a big building!"

Looking out the window and not seeing it, I knew the sedative must finally be working, so I just agreed with her while exchanging an amused look with Kosta.

After another moment of staring outside she continued, "Mommy, cars…and trees…and clouds… are buildings!"

It was interesting to listen to her chatter under the influence of a sedative. Kosta and I were nervous and tense about the procedures, but Mikayla managed to alleviate the stress somewhat as she came up with more nonsense we could laugh at.

While we were in the waiting room of the hospital, Kosta held Mikayla because she was unsteady on her feet. She was frustrated that we wouldn't let her walk around on her own and experience the odd sensation of distorted vision more fully. I had assumed the sedative would make her sleepy. If it did, she was definitely trying to fight it. She began reaching out in front of herself, her eyes slightly unfocused, attempting to grab at something that she said was the chair, which was about ten feet away.

"Mommy, I love the chairs!"

My mom joined us at the hospital and we all went in for the ultrasound around one o'clock. Mikayla was groggy, upset, and nervous. She laid down for the procedure and was interested in watching the computer screen. The ultrasound technician was cheerful and easy to be with. She had just the right amount of kindness, gentleness, and courtesy, and she kept saying how cute Mikayla was (which would automatically endear her to any mother). Mikayla was fidgety, so we tried to keep her still for the images to be clear.

The technician spent a lot of time looking at

the right-side kidney, much longer than I expected. Finally, she switched Mikayla over to the left. After considerably less time on that side, she rolled her back so she could compare images to the right side again. When she was done (after about half an hour) she said she was going to show the doctor the images and, if he wanted to see some more himself, he would be coming in.

I was not aware that this was unusual, but since my mom is a nurse, she knew that something must be wrong. She did not mention it though, as she wasn't certain and didn't want to unnecessarily alarm us. However, I could see that she was a little tense.

A doctor arrived within a few minutes. He was friendly and we liked him immediately, but then he began asking me questions that I thought had no relevance.

"Has she had blood in her urine?"

"No," I answered.

"Did her doctor feel a lump?"

What? What was he talking about? I

wondered what on earth a lump would have to do with a urinary tract infection or reflux. Was it some sort of standard question?

"No," I said again.

"Why is she here?"

Hmmm…don't you know? I thought to myself. *Isn't that listed on the intake paperwork?*

I started to feel a little frustrated. My daughter was acting upset and loopy, and now nonsensical questions were coming from a doctor who should have read the paperwork and familiarized himself with our circumstances before seeing us.

I tried to control my feelings as I told him about the kidney infection, urinary tract infections, and possible reflux. He did not respond, but instead sat down at the machine and started taking images on the right side again. The technician must have already taken a couple dozen pictures on that side alone, and I exchanged a confused look with Kosta. What was so special about that side? It was a mirror image of the left and therefore must be fine, right? We waited impatiently.

Mikayla suddenly needed to go to the bathroom again, so I picked her up and carried her to the adjoining bathroom. It was a struggle to do this with her every few minutes as I had to help her with everything while holding her upright. She was a floppy deadweight because of the sedative, and it took a lot of my strength to hold her in place.

While we were in the bathroom, I could clearly hear the doctor as he started talking to my mom and Kosta. He said that there was some sort of mass between her kidneys. As soon as I heard that sentence, I froze inside. Tears stung at my eyes and my heart started beating much faster, but I was holding Mikayla and didn't want her to see my sudden alarm.

I knew the meaning of a mass. That was usually cancer, wasn't it?

The doctor continued to discuss it, describing it as looking like a meatloaf. Great. A lump of food that Kosta can't stand eating was nestled between

Mikayla's kidneys. Was there not a better, more definitive explanation? I could feel the panic rising and quickly called my mom to come in and help Mikayla.

I went to a corner of the ultrasound room where Mikayla couldn't see me and the tears began to flow. I was desperately trying to pull myself together so that Mikayla wouldn't know I was upset. Kosta hugged me and I could see my own shock mirrored on his face. He and I were both extremely afraid of what this meant. I composed myself as my mom and Mikayla came back out, but now we had to talk to the doctor. At that moment, it was the last thing we wanted to do.

CHAPTER TWO

~ Finding The Tumor ~

"My brethren, count it all joy when ye fall into divers temptations;
knowing this, that the trying of your faith worketh patience."
~James 1:2-3

The amazing part of the story is that the doctor believed the mass to be unrelated to the kidneys. If there had not been a kidney infection or urinary tract infections to create the need for a renal ultrasound, we would not have found this potentially cancerous mass, possibly until it was too late. It was found quite by accident. The doctor thought that the mass might be attached to Mikayla's adrenal gland and had a chance of being benign, or harmless. At the time, this did not make me feel much better. Either way, there was a very large foreign object sitting inside my three-year-old. How could it be considered harmless?

The doctor still needed to perform the cystourethrogram, so he led us out to some chairs to wait for that procedure. I was completely focused on the mass and had nearly forgotten about the possible reflux.

While we were there, stressed and tense, Mikayla suddenly threw up. A large amount of juice and water went all over everything. My mom grabbed a nearby trash can but only a small amount made it inside. My mom's coat and my jeans were soaked, and it covered Mikayla's clothes. She was agitated, flailing her arms around and whimpering, still unable to stand on her own because of the sedative. We calmed her down and cleaned her up. Fortunately, I had brought a change of clothes for her, but I hadn't thought to bring one for any of the adults. We had to continue on, damp and smelly. I was relieved that we could at least make Mikayla more comfortable after that incident.

Once Mikayla had calmed down a little, we brought her to radiology; it was a big, open room that was dimly lit, with a sterile table sitting inside and covered simply with a uniform pillow and paper. There was large equipment all around the table that was a mass of black, gray, and white, humming noisily. A technician told us only two people were allowed in, so my mom went outside as we put on radiology protection vests. When he reached me, the technician asked if there was any possibility, however remote, that I could be expecting. I wasn't entirely sure, and in my hesitation, he walked me toward the door (a little too quickly) and simply said, "You can't stay."

That was it. My little girl lay agitated and whimpering on that sterile bed, and I was officially kicked out.

I went out of the room in a numb state of mind. I told my mom I wasn't allowed inside and she needed to go instead. Within moments I was alone, staring at a door that said "Radiology" above a radioactive symbol. I had only ever seen those in films, and it made me feel like we were in our own personal movie now. Unfortunately, it was a tragic drama instead of something lighthearted and happy. I closed my eyes and wished that I would wake up to find that this had all been a bad dream.

Within minutes, I heard Mikayla start to scream, making my experience seem more like a thriller. I broke down in tears, and decided to pull out my phone. For the next twenty minutes, I told a friend and my dad about the unknown mass, the fact that I wasn't allowed in the radiology room, and that my baby girl was screaming every couple of minutes. I felt helpless, knowing I couldn't comfort Mikayla through this. I had been with her every moment that morning and now she couldn't have me hold her and offer support! I was a wreck, and had no idea what was going on or why Mikayla would be screaming. Weren't they supposed to use something to assist with the catheter insertion so it wouldn't hurt? What could be wrong?

This was one of the lowest moments of my life…consumed by fear and unable to console my daughter or control what was happening to her.

During this ordeal, a nurse I did not recognize walked by, and when she saw me she said, "You're still here?" in a tone of great surprise.

At that moment, full of tension and pent-up anxiety, I was tempted to send her a dirty look and a snide retort. Obviously, we were still there. Couldn't she hear my baby crying? I settled for nodding mutely.

When the cystourethrogram finally ended, Kosta carried Mikayla out to me right away and she was crying. She wanted me to walk with her, not sit down. Apparently, the numbing agent did not work very well, so the catheter had been painful.

Mikayla had also vomited during the cystourethrogram and her second shirt was wet. She had to put on a child's hospital gown, which was soft and fuzzy with little bears and balls on it, but she was decidedly *not* happy about it. No, the bears (her favorite animal) were not cute, the gown was not fun, and it didn't matter that it was like wearing a little dress (her favorite clothing). She was *not* okay with it, and that was that. She wanted to wear her own clothes.

After a few minutes, the doctor who had read the ultrasound returned. Mikayla did not have a reflux. Finally, some good news! Of course, I would have preferred a reflux to a large, hidden mass. At least a vesicoureteral reimplantation (the reflux-corrective surgery) was an inpatient procedure that would require a hospital stay of only one or two days. Life could return to normal after something like that. Who knew how much Mikayla would be in a hospital if the mass turned out to be something harmful, or if we could return to the way life had been before the tumor was found?

Since we were there at the hospital already and the mass was confirmed, the doctor wanted to do a computed tomography (CT) scan.

Yes, yes, I thought, *just get it over with so we*

can take poor Mikayla home. She'd been through enough for one day; so had we. Every single one of us was near a breaking point.

The technician came and said that she generally doesn't allow women, other than the subject, to be present for the scan. Once more, I was kicked out. Kosta and Mikayla followed the technician into the room while my mom and I sat down and I began to cry again. I was so frustrated about not being able to be with Mikayla through everything, and I was scared of what was happening. In the space of an hour, it felt like my life had shattered. As I leaned on her shoulder and sobbed, we began to talk about what the doctors were finding. I heard my mom crying as well, and my head snapped up in surprise.

"Why are *you* crying?" I exclaimed in a panic. "You said you think the tumor is benign!"

My mom must be crying only if she was very worried. As a nurse, she had always been very straightforward and matter-of-fact about medical situations. The change in her truly unnerved me.

"Well, I do…but it's still just a lot for a little girl to deal with," she responded tearfully.

Oh, okay. So long as my mom was crying for a reason other than being worried that the mass was cancer. She was supposed to tell me that everything was just fine, wasn't she? Isn't that what mothers always do? A mother can reassure that all is well, and then the problems magically disappear, don't they? Okay, maybe I was grasping at straws, but I was really hoping for that right now. Then again, I couldn't even do the same for my own daughter at that moment.

Even in the midst of my exhausted fear, I felt so glad my mom was there. At least I had someone with me now while my daughter was in another room for an unplanned test. The morning had been a nightmare, and it wasn't even over yet. It was hard to believe that it wasn't time for bed after all we'd done and heard.

As we waited, we discussed how Mikayla

would likely need surgery to remove the mass, requiring a hospital stay of two or three days. Poor Mikayla had already spent the morning in misery! I couldn't imagine surgery. That had been my fear from the very beginning when she first had the kidney infection. My head was beginning to feel overloaded and fuzzy, and an entire world of unwelcome new things had abruptly been opened to us. There were many things to consider.

How on earth do they sedate a child enough to stay in the hospital to recover from surgery? I wondered wearily. I could not imagine Mikayla voluntarily remaining in bed, hooked up to an IV, for even one day. And anesthesia? I have never experienced that. If I had, perhaps I could be somewhat more comfortable. I would at least know what Mikayla would go through. The unknown was a frightening prospect at that moment.

Fifteen minutes later, Kosta and Mikayla returned. Unfortunately, they had not been able to do the CT scan because Mikayla could not settle down.

She was panicking, had thrown up all over Kosta, and kept yelling, "No! I said no!" The doctor said that the sedative had worn off too much and she couldn't do the scan today. By now it was about 3:30 p.m. and we had been there for almost three hours.

Our family doctor called as we were leaving and scheduled us to come in with Mikayla the following day at 11:15 a.m. We would also need to return to complete the CT scan in two days, Thursday morning. Knowing we had to return to the hospital for more tests after what we had just experienced was unnerving. I'd be separated from my daughter again while she faced large, strange, and frightening machines.

And so we left, all of us exhausted (and not smelling too good, either). Thank goodness it was over, for today at least.

Mikayla was groggy and weepy for the remainder of the day. She had double vision, but the effect wore off completely by bedtime. The first time she went to the bathroom after getting home was awful – she screamed in pain the whole time. Fortunately, the time after that was just a whimper at first, so she was beginning to heal after the catheter ordeal. However, she clung to me every time she went to the bathroom during the next twenty-four hours, afraid of having the pain she had experienced earlier.

Mikayla slept in our bed that night to ensure that she could get up on her own without stumbling. I was concerned that she might have nightmares of the procedures she had endured that day; however, she slept well and woke up around her usual time. Kosta and I, on the other hand, did not sleep well. What was happening inside our daughter's body? What bad news were we going to hear next?

I prayed more fervently than usual that evening. *Lord, please protect my daughter.* I felt like I could hardly bear to go back to a doctor tomorrow, knowing now what they would begin looking for in earnest.

Cancer.

CHAPTER THREE

~ Discoveries ~

"Seek the Lord and his strength, seek his face continually."
~1 Chronicles 16:11

October 22, 2008

After discovering the tumor, I definitely needed extra strength. By the end of the day, I was surprised that I made it through without collapsing.

Our first appointment was with our family doctor. After the startling news of a tumor the day before, and at a hospital with several unfamiliar medical personnel asking questions, it was a relief to be back in our family doctor's office (at least, as much relief as could be felt at this time). It was comforting, somehow, to be with a doctor and her staff that had known us and taken care of us for so many years. Despite the reason for our visit, we were more at ease. Instead of strangers routinely doing their job, these were people that were familiar and calming to Mikayla. They hugged us all, assured us they were praying, and gave Mikayla stickers, candy, and a pretty seashell to keep, which she loved. By the time we left, Mikayla had put half a dozen stickers on her clothing.

As our doctor examined Mikayla, she was able to just barely feel the tumor. It was well-hidden behind the kidneys and liver. Given its large size and position in the abdomen, our doctor did not want us to wait at all for further procedures to examine the mass more closely. She advised getting the CT scan done that day instead of the next. She then asked me to find family history of any inner ear, brain, or nerve cancer (neuroblastoma). No one in either of our families had those specific cancers, although my mom's family had experienced a few different types of cancer over the years.

I went through the motions in a state of numb disbelief. I never thought I'd need to find out a cancer history. The three cancers our doctor mentioned sounded pretty scary to me. Brain cancer? Nerves? I didn't think those would be the type a specialist could just cut out and then the patient would be fine again.

God, please give me strength to go through this, I prayed. Again. Or perhaps that was the tenth time by now. It didn't matter; despite whatever strength I possessed, I still needed more.

Our family doctor set up a network of other doctors for us. There would be both a pediatric oncologist and a pediatric surgeon at Providence Hospital in Anchorage where we lived. She would make an endocrinologist in Seattle aware of the situation as well. We left her office and went immediately to Providence to begin more extensive testing.

Mikayla was not at all pleased to be back at a hospital. Per the doctor's instruction, we gave her a children's dissolving Benadryl to calm her since the sedative the day before had been so hard on her. Kosta and I were running frantically around Providence to get things in order. I had to stop at radiology (there was that little radioactive symbol again) to get the liquid Mikayla needed to drink to illuminate her insides for the CT scan, and a cream to help numb her skin for the IV. We went to the lab for blood work. My mom arrived just as we went in for that and although the draw went smoothly, Mikayla screamed during the procedure and attempted to hide her arm. I didn't blame her one bit. She did not care about the band-aid either – today, Daffy Duck was not that fun.

We headed right back to radiology to do the CT scan once the blood work was done. During the half-hour wait, Mikayla stayed with Kosta to relax and calm down while my mom and I went to the cafeteria to eat something.

At this time, I experienced a very unusual feeling – I was completely disconnected from my actual body, as though I was walking around in a haze with no direction. I aimlessly moved around the cafeteria, hardly paying attention to the foods. I randomly put something on my tray and wandered over to pay for it and sit down. I ate lethargically, taking automatic bites that had truly lost their flavor. Although I was dimly aware of this strange detachment between mind and body, I couldn't pull myself out of it. My mom stayed with me, letting my mind try to absorb all the changes going on and the fears filtering through.

I managed to pull out of my odd state a little when we finished eating, and we walked back to Kosta and Mikayla. Having my own personal nurse present through all of this was wonderful; having my mom as that nurse was even better. She patiently answered my questions as we walked. It was hard to comprehend all that was happening, what each scan or blood draw was for, and what exactly the doctors were looking for. My mom was able to explain it in more understandable phrases and paint a clearer picture for me.

Mikayla was upset when we entered the room with the "big doughnut" (as we had begun to call the CT scan machine to Mikayla, since it was round like a doughnut and had a hole in the middle), though not nearly as much as she had been the previous day when she was struggling with the effects of the not-so-relaxing relaxant. She had been told that she would be going in this machine, that it wouldn't hurt, and that a really big camera would take a picture of her tummy, so she could smile for the camera. She actually managed a little smile as she laid there attempting to be relaxed and ready. It was so cute, but so sad! Even though there were many moments when she could not restrain her fear throughout this experience, she really did try so hard to be brave.

The technicians tried to put the IV in her arm but it didn't work and they injected the back of her hand instead. It was hard to explain to her that even though they put the needle in her arm, the spot wouldn't work well enough so a new place had to be used instead. She cried and had now been poked three times that day, in three different places on her arms or hands. At least now she thought the band-aids were interesting enough since there was a variety decorating her body.

I did not like this particular scan technician's demeanor. Up until this point, I had liked most of people working with us, but this one was just not that great with kids or parents. She was abrupt, impersonal, and kept saying Mikayla wouldn't be able to calm down and we shouldn't get the scan done right then. Kosta was getting frustrated as he repeated that it was urgent we get this scan done. He told her that Mikayla would do fine and we just wanted to get it finished. Though afraid, Mikayla was actually doing considerably better than the previous day. The Benadryl had made her drowsy but she did not have the loss of control over her body that had alarmed her the previous day. It was a little easier to calm her and explain what would happen.

Mikayla finally relaxed and was good about laying still. My mom and I left the room and Kosta stayed with her. Listening to the CT scan from the other side of the door was far better than the cystourethrogram experience had been. Mikayla did not cry at all, and we only heard encouraging sounds. Kosta, however, was irritated with the technician because she was not telling him and Mikayla all the information. She'd repeatedly say, "Okay, there's *one* more thing you need to do…" every few minutes. She told them they needed one picture and Mikayla instead ended up going in and out of the machine six times; so much for only "one more."

Finally, it was done. Mikayla was so proud of how brave she had been and she really wanted to go to a fun place to hang out, relax, and play without the threat of more needles hanging over her. We took her to a nearby McDonald's playland. It felt odd to be doing something so normal in the middle of all this sudden hospital activity.

However, even though she was happy to be at a playland, Mikayla missed her brother, who had always accompanied us before. She watched more than played, and after a while she said, "How about we come here different day with Taki, okay?"

What a sweetheart to remember her little brother! That melted my heart.

I called our doctor, who said that she would get the CT scan results from the hospital and call me back. We decided to stop and see some of our relatives on the way home. Mikayla was so happy to see her family; she was tired and had been poked far too many times, and she wanted to just play. She showed off her band-aids and told stories of how brave she'd been during the testing. After we visited for a few minutes, our doctor called.

Even though I was anticipating the call, I was still nervous when the phone rang. I went over to the corner of the room to speak privately. The information the doctor gave me rocked me to the core.

The lemon-sized abdominal mass described by the first doctor during the ultrasound was actually nearly twice that dimension at ten centimeters, or the size of a large mango.

Ten centimeters? How could something that size even fit inside Mikayla's petite body? My mind started racing and my heart was pounding as the doctor continued.

It looked like Mikayla had neuroblastoma, or cancer of the nerve cell, which usually originates in the adrenal gland. The mass was hidden behind the liver, kidneys, and pancreas, which was why it was harder to feel. It truly was hiding. Given that neuroblastoma has that characteristic, it is often not found until a later stage. However, we had found this quite by coincidence, and while Mikayla did not appear to be exhibiting any real symptoms yet. The doctor was encouraged by this, as it could indicate an early stage of the cancer.

Encouraging? Yes. However, at that moment I could not quite get past the *cancer* part.

I asked her to call my mom to give her the information specifically since she would be able to explain it much better than I could. By now, I had tears flowing steadily down my cheeks and I could hardly speak. Kosta could see my expression from across the room and my own dread was mirrored on his face. There were so many people who would have to be told that our little girl most likely had cancer.

When I finished the phone call, I motioned Kosta over to me and continued to cry as I told him the information the doctor had relayed. However, an odd thing happened as soon as I finished describing what was in our daughter: my tears dried up. It was as though something inside me knew I had to be strong now for my family and the others we needed to tell. My eyes still had tears in them and my voice still trembled, but I felt strength only God could have given me at that moment. My voice took on an informative recitation tone from that point onward, and remained that way whenever I had to tell someone else what was happening.

That moment began the process of telling our families and friends that Mikayla probably had cancer. As we started the information flow again, our families cried while also trying to reassure such things as they were sure Mikayla would be okay, that it may not be cancer, or that it must have been found at an early stage. Now that we were faced with cancer, we all clung desperately to the hope that the lack of symptoms indicated an early stage, despite the tumor's alarmingly large size.

It was strange how I was able to comfort others, though it felt perfectly natural. I believe that God continued to give me a calmness inside for this time – a "survival mode," as a friend later phrased it. This survival mode would be all that got me through the days to come without breaking down at every turn. I've always been a more emotionally-driven person; it truly surprised me that my mind seemed to compartmentalize what was happening and reach for information or emotion as needed.

The rest of that evening was spent on the phone. This kept us so occupied that we had no time to sit and dwell on the circumstances, to feel sorry for ourselves, to wonder if our baby girl would live. I needed to survive, to be strong for *her*. I did not want her to see me break; that would cause her more fear. I know she was already afraid and confused about what was happening. As she pointed out to me, she didn't *feel* sick, so how could she be? It was hard to explain what was happening to her in a way that she could understand. Too little information would not satisfy my intellectual child, but too much would overwhelm her with anxiety.

We asked God to guide us in what we said so that we could give Mikayla just enough, but not too much, to handle. The analogy we ended up using for her was that her body had something extra in it that shouldn't be there, like a "bad apple." We told her that the new doctors were very smart and had gone through extra schooling so that they could look at her bad apple with special pictures to see what they needed to do to fix it.

Thankfully, this explanation made sense to her now that she had something familiar she could visualize. She was less confused and more satisfied (though not happy, of course) with the information. It was heartbreaking to tell her all of this and wonder what she felt about everything happening to her. Both Kosta and I tried to be calm as we told her, but each took turns explaining as the other got teary-eyed and had to pause. Mikayla listened quietly, her lips trembling. We held her for a long time, assuring her that we loved her and at least one of us would be with her for every moment of this experience.

The responses of our family and friends were so uplifting. They gave support, encouragement, and generous offers to help in any way we needed. Many offered to pray, and then also spread the word to their friends, families, or church groups; within a short time we had people lifting up our little girl in prayer across the nation, and even further than that overseas. As we are instructed scripturally in 1 Thessalonians 5:17: "Pray without ceasing."

Without ceasing had already begun.

CHAPTER FOUR

~ Introductions ~

"Trust in the Lord with all thine heart; and lean not unto thine own understanding. In all thy ways acknowledge him, and he shall direct thy paths."
~Proverbs 3:5-6

October 23, 2008

We met with the pediatric oncologist for the first time, a completely foreign experience that we could hardly believe we needed. An oncologist. Oh, the horror. How unfair. The part of me that was tired, worn-out, and scared wanted to howl in frustration. The rational part of my mind kept reminding me how blessed we are to live in the age of such medical progress that we even have specialists like pediatric oncologists. We don't just have doctors, but doctors specifically for cancer. Even more, we have doctors specifically for cancer in *kids*. Yes, medical advancement is indeed a blessing I am thankful for. However, I'd rather feel blessed from a detached view instead of through personal experience. Unfortunately, there was nothing I could do about that.

For an entire hour before her appointment, Mikayla was whimpering that she didn't want to go back to the hospital. Our son was emotional too, from the stressful past few days and the flu. He became more attached to me than usual, and I was sad to leave him with a sitter yet again. I was a stay-at-home mom, and consequently, my kids did not have sitters on a frequent basis. He hardly saw me at all during the past two days, and I had no idea when that might change.

At the hospital, we first went to the infusion room of the pediatric oncology unit to meet the nursing staff. The infusion room is the outpatient area where children receive their treatments, whichcan last up to several hours. The first two nurses we met were very helpful and compassionate. They had both a gentleness and sweetness about them that together makes the kind of person you know you'll get along with. I had quickly learned to appreciate that type of medical professional in the past two days.

One of these ladies cheerfully showed us the room, which had a television with video games, toys, and a couple of sectioned-off cubicles set up for the patients. It was bright and inviting. The first hint of what the room's purpose was came when I noticed a container of hats sitting in a basket on the check-in counter. They were mostly handmade donations knitted in a rainbow of colors, the girls' ones adorned with pretty ribbons or flowers. I steeled myself against the thought that perhaps Mikayla would need one soon to warm her head where hair had once been…before chemotherapy changed it all.

One child was in the infusion room already, a small boy with no hair who was receiving his chemotherapy treatment through an IV attached to a line in his chest. This particular kind of line is an intravenous catheter inserted through the chest wall to the main vein carrying blood from the body to the heart. The line remains long-term for the administration of chemotherapy and prevents the patient from needing an injection every time a new treatment is performed. Seeing it for the first time really shook me up. The boy, however, didn't seem to mind it and continued playing a video game as though he were at home and not at the hospital receiving chemotherapy for cancer. He must have been only a year or so older than Mikayla and I almost couldn't bear to look at him, knowing that it could soon be my own daughter seated there.

After the tour, we went upstairs to the doctor's office. Even though I knew we would be back, I felt a keen sense of relief as the door to the infusion room closed firmly behind us. The five minutes we spent there already felt like too much. Both my mom and her husband met us in the doctor's office and we were glad for the support as well as the distraction for Mikayla. They entertained her as she clung to Kosta while we waited for the doctor. She was nervous and cried when the nurse placed a thermometer under her arm to take her temperature and also as the blood pressure cuff was wrapped around her arm.

We liked the doctor very much. He was gentle and soft-spoken, and Mikayla was able to relax around him. My mom wrote down most of what the doctor told us, which was helpful for me. I had a lot of people to relay information to and the new terms were hard to remember. The oncologist said he did not want to rush to a diagnosis of neuroblastoma yet, but needed to run more tests to rule out other possibilities. One was just a simple urinalysis, and Mikayla had no problem with that. She was also extremely relieved when the doctor assured her that he himself wouldn't poke her at all; the nurses are always assigned to that unhappy task. I would think they must be trained specifically on how to draw blood from a panicked and combative child who might refuse to relinquish any access to veins. It certainly could not be a fun part of the job.

After we finished our meeting with the oncologist, we met with the pediatric surgeon. The wait in a room took nearly an hour, and during that time Mikayla was energetic and silly. Two hours in a hospital without receiving a shot really boosted her confidence. She had fun playing with all the toys and getting on the exam table. There was a child's doctor set in the room, and Mikayla gave her parents and grandparents at least two injections each with the plastic syringe. Her teddy bear got it several times more than the rest of us. Mikayla was definitely enjoying administering shots instead of receiving them. I was really tired by now and after awhile I laid on the table to rest, which convinced Mikayla that I needed more shots.

When the surgeon arrived, however, all playfulness stopped immediately. Mikayla backed away from the man and climbed into Kosta's lap, curling into a ball in an attempt to make herself as inconspicuous as possible. When he assured her that he would not poke her with a needle, she ventured a look in his direction and relaxed marginally.

The surgeon, like the oncologist, had a quiet personality, and he was very informative. He began a new onslaught of information and when I turned to ask my mom if she could take notes again, I saw that she had already begun. The surgeon had seen the CT scan and immediately began to describe possible scenarios, outlining the process on a small notepad. He explained that the tumor, at ten centimeters, was too big to remove easily and needed to be shrunk first.

Aside from the large size, another significant problem was that the tumor was wrapped around the celiac and hepatic arteries and needed to release its hold on those blood vessels in order to be removed. The celiac artery stems from the abdominal aorta and supplies oxygenated blood to the liver and other organs. The hepatic artery is a branch of the celiac artery which also carries blood to the organs. If they attempted to remove the tumor as it was, it would not be a simple matter of going in and pulling it out – it would have to be scraped carefully from each branched artery it wrapped around. Chemotherapy, on the other hand, would reduce the tumor's size and possibly cause it to pull away from the arteries.

The doctor went on to say that the tumor was concealed in part behind the liver, pancreas, and kidneys, and was large enough that it crossed over the center line (the middle point of the body). Further tests would be needed to determine the grade and stage of cancer. Grading is done by a scale of one through three, with one indicating a slow-growing tumor and three indicating fast growth. Staging refers to the severity of cancer based on the tumor's characteristics and whether or not the cancer has spread anywhere else in the body.

Neuroblastoma can spread to the lymph nodes, liver, or bones. Stages 1 and 2A would indicate a tumor that has not yet crossed the center line of the body. My brief hope of a stage 1A cancer diagnosis was extinguished quickly and my stress level began to rise. Because Mikayla's tumor was large enough to have already crossed that point, the doctor indicated that he believed her to be closer to the 2B stage, and he wouldn't necessarily expect stage 3 because Mikayla was not symptomatic. I wasn't sure which was more concerning – the tumor's wrap around major arteries, or the sheer size of it. Both were very alarming.

Because of the size of the tumor, the doctor said it would most likely be malignant (containing deadly cancer cells). However, since Mikayla had no symptoms yet, he thought it possible that at least some of the tumor could be benign (not containing cancer cells). An open biopsy would be performed, with a surgeon making an incision large enough to find the tumor and extract pieces from different parts. Then these pieces would be tested by a pathologist to determine if any parts were benign or if all of it was malignant.

My mind rebelled at the word *malignant*. It should not have been used in the same sentence as my daughter's name. Didn't anyone realize that?

We were told that if the tumor contained any malignant cells, Mikayla would need to have chemotherapy for at least six months and possibly up to two years, depending on the stage of the cancer. She would also have the open biopsy, a bone marrow biopsy, and a positron emission tomography scan (PET scan) of the whole body to determine if the cancer had spread anywhere else. Once the mass had shrunk enough through the chemotherapy, it would be removed by a surgeon.

My stress level skyrocketed, and a panicked chant began running through my mind. *Cancer, cancer, cancer.*

The surgeon informed us that a tumor board, comprised of physicians in five northwestern states who met every Tuesday morning by phone, would be reviewing Mikayla's case to determine the course of treatment. We would need to go to Seattle for further testing, some or all of the needed procedures, and to begin chemotherapy. The board would determine what could be done in Seattle and what procedures/treatments, if any, could be done in Anchorage where we lived.

A small piece of good news was that the tumor did not appear to be obstructing other organs. I wondered how such a large tumor managed to fit inside my petite daughter without causing problems for us to notice. It hardly seemed possible, but apparently there's enough room inside to squeeze an extra part in and squish everything closer with no notice to the rest of the body.

The doctor instructed us that even though Mikayla was asymptomatic, the tumor was large and needed to not be bumped at all. This translated to no ballet (which she'd participated in for nearly a year), rough-housing (that would be hard with two small children), jumping off things (try telling that to a three-year-old), or falling down (the only way to guarantee that would be to carry her everywhere). She should wear shoes on slippery floors to avoid a potential fall.

After this informative but energy-depleting

meeting concluded, we returned to the infusion room for more blood work. Kosta and I had been dreading this part, knowing it was the hardest thing for Mikayla to endure. We both stayed for the blood draw, and my mom and stepdad waited in a "safe room" – a room where they never perform tests that cause pain. I personally felt that a "safe room" must imply that there is a "not-so-safe room" somewhere. I would think that kids might panic and know what was coming, but perhaps it does help many kids as intended. Mikayla, however, would definitely be the type to panic as she approached the not-so-safe room.

The nurses in the infusion ward generally do well with the blood draw. A Child Life specialist comes in with fun distractions for the patient in an attempt to divert the attention from what is about to happen. However, even with that, Mikayla's draw was awful – the worst she had experienced so far. They used a vein in the back of her right hand that looked full enough for easy access.

Sterilize…poke…insert…and no blood came

out.

They began moving the needle around a little, trying to get the blood. Mikayla, poor girl, screamed continually. It felt like five minutes before they managed to get any blood from the vein. Mikayla kept screaming as Kosta held her tightly in place and I leaned over her, my hand stroking her face as I spoke soothingly, though I think she was past the point of hearing anything I said. When I saw that no blood was forthcoming and my precious daughter continued crying, I began to cry as well, though I tried hard to hold it back. It was so awful to see my daughter go through that trauma yet again.

Lord, please hold me steady. I'm about to lose it.

They finally got the blood and finished. Mikayla's hand was bruised and bleeding still, so they had to wrap it instead of using the usual band-aid. She had really wanted a band-aid this time, so they showed her all of them and she picked out a rainbow-patterned one to decoratively put on top of the bandage wrap. I couldn't stop the tears that kept streaming down my cheeks and didn't want her to see me that way, so my mom and Kosta stayed with Mikayla, and my stepdad comforted me until I managed to calm down. Mikayla wanted me to take a picture so I could show people how brave she had been. She posed with her rainbow band-aid and a tragic-but-adorable sort of grimace in place of her usual sunny smile.

Finally, we were done. When we picked up our son and headed home, we were again on the phone continually to give explanations to everyone. Preparations to leave for Seattle would need to begin.

CHAPTER FIVE

~ Getting Ready To Leave ~

"Be careful for nothing; but in everything by prayer and supplication with thanksgiving let your requests be made known unto God. And the peace of God, which passeth all understanding, shall keep your hearts and minds through Christ Jesus."
~Philippians 4:6-7

October 24, 2008

Kosta and I had to make a decision about the pending trip to Seattle. Do we all go? Should only our son stay home in the care of our family members? But he was only two years old and quite attached to me. He'd never been away from me for longer than two nights. We did not want to split our family at such a traumatic time, but we also did not know what to expect, nor did we have any indication of how long we would be gone. The doctors had implied an absence of at least ten days to two weeks

– enough time to complete the round of tests needed as well as the biopsies, and to receive the first chemotherapy treatment. However, they also mentioned the possibility of being in Seattle for months if the tumor board decided that the Seattle Children's Hospital should oversee all of Mikayla's treatments.

We finally decided that I would initially accompany Mikayla and Kosta would stay behind with our son. If Mikayla and I were gone for more than a week or two, they would come down to visit for a few days, and we could then discuss what to do. After a week or so, we would most likely know what was happening and where Mikayla needed to be.

We were waiting to hear from a social worker, who was responsible for arranging our travel. At this point, I had no idea which day we would leave. I set about doing laundry and tried to start packing, but it was very difficult. Everything unsure and indefinite, and I struggled with not knowing what was going on. Should I pack for one week or four?

Would Mikayla need much clothing, or would she be confined to a little hospital gown continually? Should chemotherapy begin, I had no idea if she would be in the hospital all the time or just return periodically to receive a treatment and then leave again. Did people in our predicament have to leave their jobs or schools indefinitely? What about paying the monthly bills? All these things went through my mind and that feeling of overwhelming despair returned.

Compartmentalize, I reminded myself. *One thing at a time*.

The call from the social worker came late that day and he had scheduled Mikayla and I to leave the following Monday. Insurance would cover the cost of travel, lodging, and meals for both of us. He would call back again with the precise arrangements. Now that I knew exactly when the separation of my family would occur, I became more emotional and it was harder to focus. I cried off and on, and gradually grew more and more irritable.

Our airline tickets were purchased as one-way. What a nightmare. I wasn't even gone yet and I already wanted to go *home*.

We went to a toy store and Mikayla picked out some fun things to take with us to Seattle. We told her that she and mommy would be taking a special trip to see some doctors at a different hospital. Outwardly, Kosta and I remained positive, telling Mikayla that her daddy and brother would stay home but that we would still be able to do fun, special things in Seattle, even though we would also have to go to the hospital.

Mikayla enjoyed getting new things to bring along and was distracted for the time being. There wasn't much else to do for her; pray, hug, distract…and repeat. Though this was a terrible thing to have to endure at age three, there was one small advantage – she was too young to truly understand everything and fear the test results or her own mortality as an older child might. Mikayla would even forget much of what she went through, depending on the duration of her ordeal. It was a small comfort…but a comfort nonetheless.

I, however, was not doing so well. I would forget nothing.

When we returned home, I went into our bedroom and cried. For nearly half an hour, it all came out in a wave of emotion as Kosta held me. I was afraid of the impending separation and didn't want to be without my husband as our daughter was treated for cancer. I didn't know how to leave my two-year-old son for an indefinite period of time. The word *unfair* entered my mind for what felt like the thousandth time, and I prayed for more strength.

October 25, 2008

Of all things to happen this day, two days before our departure, Kosta woke up with stomach flu. I couldn't believe it. I had subconsciously figured that if we were fighting something like cancer, we would be exempt from everyday illnesses. Now I wondered how I could get everything done in time. Kosta spent most of the day resting and was frustrated that he had to stay away from all of us, especially Mikayla. Fortunately, others offered to help me take care of things that needed to be done. My close friend volunteered to run to the store for me since I did not have time to go out. She wrote down a list and showed up with everything less than two hours later.

My mom had just left town for a business trip, but she planned to meet us in Seattle the following Thursday, which would be three days into our trip. My stepdad came over that evening with dinner cooked for us by a friend of theirs, which was another great blessing. He then went to a bookstore and picked up a paperback set of my favorite book series so that I could take it along with me and not be carrying the heavier hardback copies. He also got some photo paper so I could make a book of family photographs to take with us. Mikayla was especially excited about this, and loved her own little book of family pictures that she could now carry everywhere.

In addition to doing those things for us, just

having my stepdad with us that day was a great comfort. He played with the kids, offered reassurance and optimism, and discussed cancer and the upcoming tests. His presence that evening was invaluable and he stayed to help and be with us for the entire evening. My sister called and stopped by our house just to give me a hug, and her comfort was also greatly appreciated.

The worst frustration of the day was my experience with the social worker. He called early in the afternoon to go over the finalized travel plans. He had purchased the airline tickets for a flight departure of 2:30 p.m. on Monday, and had also arranged a one-night stay at the Seattle Ronald McDonald House.

One night? But our tickets were one-way! We would be there indefinitely, for several nights at least, considering that a biopsy was scheduled. There was no way we would be in and out again in just one day. He assumed we would be staying at the hospital and I told him we had no idea of any of these plans, and would not know anything for sure until Tuesday when we were to go to the hospital. What was I supposed to do with our luggage? He suggested I bring it to the hospital and stow it in an office somewhere. I would have laughed if I weren't so close to tears.

I had not been given any information from anyone yet about what it would be like at the hospital or what was available for a child's parent. I felt like I was walking forward in a pitch-black tunnel without a light. I had no idea what to expect. Under the circumstances, perhaps his arrangements were appropriate, but by this time I was not running on a consistent meter of reasonability. I felt that we needed a place to shower, store our things, and rest. I also reminded him that my husband and son would be coming down for days at a time, and would join us permanently if it turned out that we needed to stay until all chemotherapy treatments were completed. He ended up agreeing with me, but said that the insurance had authorized one night and he'd have to call again to authorize more.

I decided to call both the Ronald McDonald House and the airline to confirm the reservations. I had read on the House's website that a stay there was required to be four nights at a minimum, so I wondered if the social worker had actually spoken to them at all yet.

I called the House to ask if someone there had talked with our social worker.

No, they had not. I wasn't surprised.

The woman I spoke to was wonderful. She was no doubt used to irate and panicky parents. She wrote down our information to put us on a waiting list since there was no availability at that moment. (No room available? What? My panic started rising again. Where would we stay for an indefinite period of time?) The woman told me that there was no way to estimate when a room would become available, though when we got one we would have it until we decided to leave. When the House assigns a room to a family, it is theirs for as long as they need it, which is one of the many great things about the Ronald McDonald House Charities organization. They know a family may need a place to stay for two days, two months, or even two years. They have additional long-term housing for the families whose child needed a bone marrow transplant.

When I called the airline next, they confirmed that a reservation had been made. Well, at least that one really had been done.

The social worker called me back and I told him of my conversation with the Ronald McDonald House, that I had put myself on the waiting list. He had not yet been able to reach the insurance to authorize additional days of lodging, but the office would open again the next day at noon. Since there were two hotels that accepted payment by insurance, we would potentially be at one of those for one night, so at least we wouldn't fly into Seattle without a place to go upon arrival. I felt only marginally better. Now we were praying that the housing dilemma would resolve quickly so that I could feel more secure when we arrived in Seattle.

CHAPTER SIX

~ Saying Goodbye ~

"How excellent is thy lovingkindness, O God! Therefore the children of men put their trust under the shadow of thy wings. They shall be abundantly satisfied with the fatness of thy house; and thou shalt make them drink of the river of thy pleasures. For with thee is the fountain of life: in thy light shall we see light."
~Psalm 36:7-9

October 26, 2008

The Ronald McDonald House had an opening! Oh, joy! We would have a place to stay for as long as we were there. I felt much better. When the social worker called us with the news, I called the House to confirm the arrangement. Knowing we had a room reserved for us until whenever we were cleared to return to Alaska made me feel so much more secure. Kosta and Taki would be able to visit us without worrying about lodging.

In addition to the good news about housing, Kosta also felt better and his symptoms had abated. We discussed how to bridge the separation of our family, and agreed to not be apart longer than two weeks at a time. Kosta would fly down with our son to see us for two or three days every two weeks so long as Mikayla and I were in Seattle, and from time to time we would switch places so that Kosta could be with Mikayla and Taki could spend a longer period of time with me.

We worried about the travel cost, but agreed that seeing each other was more important. Their first trip down would be in eleven days. We had a companion coupon to use through Alaska Airlines, minimizing the cost of that first trip, and some family and friends blessed us by offering frequent flier miles for future trips. We were very touched by that generosity. I planned to take a laptop along, and with the webcam it had we would be able to have daily visual phone conversations.

Family began to come over to say good-bye.

This was especially heart-wrenching, as we did not know when we would return or what Mikayla's condition would be at that time. Would she already have been through several rounds of chemotherapy? Would she be sick, pale, and thinner than usual? Would her hair fall out?

Our family hugged her tightly, wondering, I am sure, when they would see her next. The family members who lived nearby had seen Mikayla regularly throughout her entire life. Even though she might return within a week or two, how sad it was to know that it could actually stretch out to six months or more!

My sister came over with her family, bringing along lunch for us, and my stepdad stopped by again. It was probably good that our families kept reminding us to eat. It had definitely become less of a priority to both Kosta and I in the past several days, and we might have forgotten some meals entirely had people not brought food.

I had started packing and one of the first

things I realized was that our suitcases weren't large enough. My stepdad and brother-in-law immediately went out and purchased us a new set of luggage, and they picked up my travel information and vouchers from the hospital. My sister stayed and cleaned up the kitchen, then helped me pack. I kept trying to put off the packing. It made everything so much more definite in my mind. However, as we were scheduled to leave early the next day, I couldn't put it off any longer.

By the time everyone left that evening, my son was acting grumpy and was not his usual, cheerful self. I was worried that he was getting a cold. The four of us watched Disney's *Hercules* together and then we put the kids to bed. I spent ten minutes singing to Taki while Kosta read Bible stories to Mikayla. It was my last night with my son, and Kosta's last night with his daughter. I looked in on Mikayla when she was asleep and sat down on her bed, simply watching her breathe peacefully. Her fourth birthday was right around the corner. One part of me wondered if we would be home for it after all. The other part of me (the one I tried frequently to ignore during this ordeal) wondered if four would be the last birthday we would get to celebrate with her.

After the kids were asleep, Kosta and I spent time talking and crying together. He was a great strength and comfort to me, and I was discouraged in knowing that soon Mikayla and I would be leaving without him.

October 27, 2008

Taki was up frequently throughout the night, which was unusual. He definitely had a cold now, so in addition to worrying about him being sick and not having mommy there to care for him, I was also concerned that I would get it and be separated from Mikayla, since those with respiratory illnesses are not allowed in the pediatric oncology ward at a hospital. Children with cancer are more susceptible to illnesses, so the ward is kept as clean and germ-free as possible. Kosta continued to be strong and reassuring. He has always been a wonderful, loving, involved father, and I felt better knowing that he would take the best care of Taki in my absence. At least one parent would still be there for our sweet little boy.

Kosta's family came over to say goodbye and Mikayla got several hugs from her grandparents, uncle, aunt, and cousin. Although she was excited to go on a special airplane trip, Mikayla was disappointed to be leaving that day because her cousin was having a birthday party in the evening and Mikayla had been looking forward to it. Now she would have to miss all the fun of playing with her cousin and instead be getting ready to go to a hospital.

As we drove to the airport, I frequently glanced back at Taki. I missed him already. It was a struggle for Kosta and me to hug our children goodbye, but I was determined to not cry in front of Mikayla the entire time we were gone. I did not want to add to her stress and hoped that she would only see me being strong and positive.

Mikayla loved the whole airplane trip experience. She watched planes from our gate and got a window seat once we boarded our plane. She spent the half hour before take-off looking at all the planes and baggage cars she saw outside of her window. The lift-off was especially exciting for her, watching the ground get farther and farther away, and then she took out some of her new books and stickers. There was no one else in our row, so we had three seats to ourselves. After eating lunch (yet another fascinating experience for a toddler on an airplane), Mikayla curled up on my lap and took a nap.

My aunt and uncle met us at the airport and drove us to the Ronald McDonald House. Having family meet us was such a blessing, as it was difficult for me to manage our luggage as well as Mikayla, who was wanting to be carried more than usual after the hospital trials began. I was worn out and down-hearted, and I appreciated having family with us to help ease the burden both physically and emotionally.

The Ronald McDonald House facilities in Seattle are wonderful. There are a few separate housing sites, each with activities, laundry, a large kitchen and dining area, and living room. All are well-kept and there is on-site staff to welcome newcomers, give a tour, and oversee things.

Unfortunately, my temporary optimism was dashed when I noticed that our room had two twin beds. I had forgotten to specify a request for a room with two larger double beds and, upon seeing the twins, my heart sank. Where would Kosta and Taki sleep when they came to be with us? Also, at this point, with the excitement of the trip wearing off, Mikayla was scared of what she would face at the hospital the next day. This caused her to become very clingy and she adamantly insisted that she be able to sleep with me. I pushed the beds together, but it was an uncomfortable night. Mikayla took hours to fall asleep, and it was well past midnight when she finally did, her little hand holding mine. I tossed and turned, my mind filled with thoughts of home and what to expect at the hospital the next day.

At five in the morning, I gave up trying to sleep. Mikayla woke up around seven, and my aunt and uncle drove us to the hospital by eight, which was an early start to what was most likely going to be a long, miserable day.

CHAPTER SEVEN

~ The Ordeal ~

"I will not leave you comfortless: I will come to you."
~John 14:18

October 28, 2008

My lack of sleep made things harder, but the best thing about this day was that my aunt and uncle stayed with us at the hospital. I don't know how I would have made it through otherwise. God truly placed some special people in our lives to help us endure this experience. I was never without the presence of a family member or friend while in Seattle except for during the nights. Each person was a much-needed blessing and comfort for me.

Mikayla was tired, scared, whiny, and clingy.

I was probably worse, though in a relatively silent manner. I had to carry Mikayla everywhere in the hospital, so my uncle kindly carried our things. We'd come equipped with a backpack of activities for Mikayla, and I traveled with a large binder and notebook to jot down what the doctors were saying, as well as my purse. Combined with our coats, it was a lot of stuff. He shouldered the burden without complaint and I just had to carry Mikayla.

Our first stop was a blood draw. This is what I had been dreading the most.

When Mikayla realized what was going to happen, she completely panicked. The lab technician and I had to wrestle her arm away from her body, where she was clenching it tightly. She screamed the entire time and continued for an additional five minutes after it was over. Once she calmed down, I carried her up to the oncologist's office, where they told us we had to go back downstairs for a chest and neck x-ray. Mikayla was very afraid of this new machine, even though we told her there would be no pokes. Despite that reassurance, my poor little girl was quivering from head to toe. The technicianallowed me to stand with her and hold her arms up for the clear picture.

We went back to the oncologist's office and waited. At that time, they told us that Mikayla could not have any more food or drink because they had scheduled a CT scan for the afternoon. I felt terrible about this, as she was already hungry and asking for something to eat.

Our new oncologist repeated much of the same information we already knew. He explained that we would be doing the CT scan and then Mikayla would be admitted after that. The surgeon would come to see us in our room either tonight or tomorrow morning to discuss and schedule the biopsies.

Unfortunately, we now had to go back downstairs to get the IV set up for the CT scan. Knowing that an injection was coming again, I was extremely apprehensive. I wondered how much more

Mikayla could take. She was already tired, hungry, and cranky, and it wasn't even noon. Once Mikayla got the IV, it would be another two or three hours of waiting until the scan could be done. Since she didn't know she was getting an injection, she was able to relax somewhat as she colored pictures in a notebook. It was a relief to me that three-year-olds are semi-distractible. Mikayla was functioning on a series of highs and lows. The happiness caused from circumstances such as, *Oh fun, a new book!* was inevitably followed by the trauma of, *Another stranger wants to stab me with a sharp needle!*

Though I delighted in watching Mikayla during these highs, I was always the one that had to interrupt her worry-free time and break it to her that it was time for the next round of poking. Every time I did that, her reaction got worse. This moment was no exception. She screamed, hid her hands and adamantly yelled, "No!"

It was, by far, her absolute worst reaction to an injection. The nurses gave her a numbing agent before the IV, but it was administered by a syringe that made a loud blasting noise, which terrified Mikayla even more. She became combative, making it hard to get her hand still enough to administer the IV.

When it was finally finished (after several agonizing minutes that included a violent tantrum and a full set of fifty colored pencils scattered all over the floor), the nurse gave Mikayla a little Sleeping Beauty lunchbox, which she tearfully accepted. Though Mikayla was never a mean or rough child by any means, I'm pretty sure that at that moment she was seriously contemplating throwing the lunch box at the woman. Then again, perhaps God was touching Mikayla's heart with an extra dose of love and endurance, for I never saw her become angry with any of the medical professionals she encountered over the course of this entire ordeal. Though she fought against the administration of needles or attempted to escape, she never once directed her distress specifically to a nurse or doctor.

We had some time now before the scheduled scan, so I told Mikayla we would go to the gift shop where she could pick something out. She wandered around the shop with interest, finally choosing a stuffed polar bear that wore a blue *Children's Hospital* shirt.

My aunt suggested that we take Mikayla to one of the hospital's playrooms, which I didn't even know existed. The room was amazing – a large, colorful area filled with books, toys, play tables, movies, video games, and other entertainment for all ages. Mikayla played for about forty-five minutes, looking tragically adorable as she carefully held her IV-wrapped hand. There was a fun-looking playground right outside the room that Mikayla wanted to go out to, but it had been raining and all the equipment was wet. I hovered close to her, remembering the surgeon's warning to not allow Mikayla to fall or get bumped.

When it was time, we took Mikayla down to the CT scan room, where she recognized the "big doughnut" machine, this one decorated with a large variety of fun stickers that Mikayla enjoyed looking at. I held her as they began to inject the anesthesia through the IV. Mikayla was afraid of this unfamiliar white liquid, and I reassured her that it would not cause any pain, that it was just like lotion that would go inside her body. She wasn't quite so afraid.

At that time, one of the lab technicians warned me that it could be disturbing for the parent to watch how quickly the anesthesia worked. I thought it would be a *relief* at this point, not a concern. Considering how scared she had been all morning, I was looking forward to her taking a medicine-induced nap during a procedure instead of being awake. However, when Mikayla immediately went completely limp and fell into that deep sleep, it was indeed a shock. My child was suddenly still and nonresponsive. I laid her back on the table and the sight of her so motionless, with a small sliver of white showing beneath her eyelids, suddenly choked me up. I couldn't help crying at that point, knowing that Mikayla couldn't see me.

My aunt and uncle led me out and brought me to the cafeteria, as it had been nearly eight hours since I had last eaten. Fortunately, they had the presence of mind to follow the hospital map we had been given upon our arrival. I was hardly able to pay attention to anything and would surely have remained lost for a long time. I was, yet again, thankful for the family so willing to help me when I needed them the most.

There was some confusion in getting to the room where Mikayla would be admitted. The hospital had shuffled us around so rapidly that day that a file had not yet been made. Finally, we were taken to the Seattle Cancer Care Alliance Unit, Hematology/Oncology ward. Mikayla's hospital room was shared with a teenage girl accompanied by her mother, but she was discharged that same evening. After that, we had no roommates. I know it's good that many hospital rooms are designed for double occupants, but I was grateful for the extra space and privacy at this time.

Mikayla was wheeled into the room on a hospital crib bed. Her eyes were open and she was groggy and weepy, calling out for me in a drugged-sounding voice. She held out her arms and I picked her up and carried her to the bed. She didn't want me to let go of her, so I stayed there and held her. She was very agitated and demanding while I spoke with the nurses. If she said my name and I did not immediately respond, she got angry.

Over the next half hour Mikayla remained on edge, sometimes even hitting me or yelling. My little girl had never done anything like that to me – to *anyone* – before, and I was taken aback. I hardly knew how to handle it. The nurse told me that it wasn't uncommon behavior for a child coming out of anesthesia. I could barely stand it and held her while shaking and crying silently, the tears running from my cheeks into her tangled hair. I simply could not hold the emotion back any longer and kept Mikayla cradled snugly to my chest so she would not see my face.

Once the nurse turned the room's television on to a cartoon channel, Mikayla finally began to calm down and rest. I continued to cry silently for nearly twenty minutes as I held her. For the rest of the evening, Mikayla watched movies as people came and went. She was hungry by now and cleared to eat whatever she felt like, so she kept requesting toast. The nurses brought more toast every twenty minutes or so, and Mikayla ate six whole slices, crackers, and drank a lot of milk by the time she was satiated. She had always been a petite child on the lower end of the weight percentile chart, and I worried that days of eating so little would drop her weight even more. It was reassuring to see her eat so much that evening.

My cousin who lived nearby came to see us. He and his wife brought books for Mikayla to help occupy her time. By the time our visitors left, I was exhausted. I slept in Mikayla's hospital bed with her because she was too nervous to be by herself. We read some of the books and talked with Kosta on the computer that my uncle had so kindly set up for us with the internet connection. It was so heartbreaking for Kosta to see Mikayla in the hospital bed, connected to an IV, and not be able to be with her.

It took over an hour for Mikayla to fall asleep once we turned the light off, which was an improvement from the previous night. I slept very little, as the bed was cramped and uncomfortable with two of us on it, and I continually awakened at Mikayla's slightest movement. There were several times that she rolled toward me, put her arm around me, and snuggled closer. She felt so small and fragile, even more than usual.

I noticed an unfamiliar odor on her and was later told that it was the scent of anesthesia. To me she smelled like a hospital, and it meant that something was wrong. It only served to make me hold her closer. With her safely asleep, I could cry as much as I needed to. Though I had cried off and on throughout the day, I had still attempted to conceal my tears and hold back the flood of emotion hovering on the edge. Now, however, the weight of the day pressed upon me like a boulder and my emotions were stretched to breaking point.

Up to this point, the day we learned about the tumor was the worst I could have imagined, and each subsequent day was extremely stressful; but this day felt like my hardest so far. With surgery still to come, results to hear, and treatments to be given, I knew that worse was yet to come. I felt I could hardly withstand any more of the trials that had been abruptly placed before us.

As Mikayla slept peacefully, held in a protective embrace, I felt the weight of the world upon my own shoulders. New tears traced the hours-old tracks down my face and dampened the hospital pillow.

Lord, let me wake up and find this was just a nightmare, I prayed silently. My monotonous desperate plea was repeated for several minutes before the panicked fog of that thought could begin to clear from my mind. Gradually it was replaced with a new request.

Please walk me through this, Lord.

I have always been the type of person to plan ahead, organizing and detailing everything. However, this situation was different. At that moment, it was all almost completely unable to be planned. There was nothing I could do to map it out, organize it…control it.

The unknown.

I might as well have been in a dark abyss at the bottom of the ocean.

Fear.

Yes, it ran through my entire being at regular intervals. I found that when I was busy and focused on Mikayla, I could bury it for that moment. However, it was always just below the surface. In the still, silent moments, it would return. On this first night in the hospital, away from home and my husband, with surgery and doctors and more unfamiliar terms only hours away, the fear resurfaced.

But not for God, I realized.

No, he knew Mikayla's body inside when I did not. Doctors would need to search for answers and I would have to wait to hear them, but God would not. There was no fear for him.

Lord, I need your strength.

I needed strength like I needed oxygen. At that moment, I focused all of my energy on my prayer for strength and peace. The deep abyss in my own personal ocean changed just a little.

I had a light.

It wasn't the giant searchlight I preferred, but it was still a light. It was enough – just enough to see where to put my next step. God was filling me with enough peace to last me step by step, moment by moment. I needed strength just to get through another day, and when that day was over and a new one began, I would need more strength to start again. At moments like these, when my frail human strength crumbled faster than usual, God could fill me anew.

CHAPTER EIGHT

~ Surgery Day ~

*"For I know the thoughts that I think toward you, saith the Lord,
thoughts of peace, and not of evil, to give you an expected end."*
~Jeremiah 29:11

October 29, 2008

I got up for the day by eight and Mikayla awakened an hour later. A nurse told me that Mikayla's surgery was to be at 10:30 a.m. Although I was terrified, it was still good to know the surgery would be soon since she again had to fast. Mikayla wanted more toast, but had to hear once more that she couldn't eat because of another procedure.

My aunt and uncle had left the evening before, but I was not alone for longer than it took to wake up. Another aunt, as well as a very good friend of mine and Kosta's, arrived right after we got up. This aunt was also a nurse, like my mom and other aunt that had been with me the previous day. In addition to her comforting presence, it was very reassuring and helpful to have a nurse with me on surgery day. Our friend was also a welcome support who managed to get Mikayla to smile from time to time.

The scheduled surgery time of 10:30 came and went, and then another hour went by. A nurse came in to tell us there was a delay. They now hoped the surgery would be able to start at 12:30 p.m. Unfortunately, that time also passed. Two Child Life specialists came in to explain what was going to occur. They brought along some props to illustrate to Mikayla what would happen in the surgery. I was wary but curious. How can you illustrate a serious surgery to a three-year-old?

By using their helpful little stuffed friend, Chemo Duck, of course.

I have to admit that Chemo Duck was adorable. He was perhaps ten inches tall, white and fluffy with a yellow bill and even wearing a blue doctor's scrub complete with a little face mask. The only thing missing was a miniature stethoscope. He was like a doctor's dream version of the plush Easter duckies we see crowding out the bunnies in the seasonal aisle in March.

But Chemo Duck had one big drawback – a piece of the outfit on his chest had a flap that could open. When the Child Life specialist pulled the flap back, it revealed a Hickman catheter line that had been inserted in little Chemo Duck's chest.

My eyes widened with alarm, but before I could think to interfere, they explained to Mikayla that she'd go into a special sleep and get to come out just like Chemo Duck with a funny little magic tube in *her* chest, and isn't that silly?

Oh, my goodness. No, no, no!

And unfortunately, Mikayla agreed with my silent assessment – it was *not* silly, not one single bit. She wailed in terror.

"Noooooo, I don't want that in me!"

Seriously; who could blame her?

Maybe our fuzzy little friend Chemo Duck works on other children. However, it's not the kind of visual prop that would work on this particular three-year-old. Mikayla has always had a very good visual memory, and she was not at all impressed with anything related to the hospital or the changes which would be made to her body.

Chemo Duck had to go.

I hastened to intervene, cradling Mikayla (who was now bawling steadily) and blocking Chemo Duck from view. Not wanting to be rude, I simply told the Child Life specialist that it was okay and Mikayla would be fine. The specialist looked chagrined and left, telling me she would be back to help later. As soon as she was gone, I assured Mikayla that Chemo Duck would not return, and stuffed the offending prop deep into the cabinet.

After Mikayla calmed down, the nurse explained the rest to us that Mikayla would have a biopsy of the tumor done, which would leave a two-

or three-inch scar diagonally along the right side of her abdomen. She would undergo a bone marrow biopsy, which would leave two small "pencil mark" scars on her lower back on each side of the base of her spine (for reference, they turned out slightly bigger than *my* idea of a pencil mark; maybe she meant one of those extra-thick pencils with a dulled tip and not a standard-sized sharpened pencil). The Hickman catheter would also be inserted into her chest, leaving a hole with a tube in it that would be used to administer chemotherapy.

Oh no, I thought. *Everything at once? Sore back, chest, and abdomen at the same time?*

I was horrified and overwhelmed. I was also ready to destroy, de-stuff, or do whatever was needed to permanently remove Chemo Duck from memory.

Now, don't get me wrong. I am profoundly grateful for the advances we have made in medicine. Where we are now, in the twenty-first century, is absolutely remarkable. At the time of my childhood, I would not have gotten a Hickman catheter in my chest. No, I'd have had to get poked every single time I needed a chemotherapy treatment. I was extremely relieved that Mikayla, who was obviously terrified of needles by this point, would not need to get poked again after this. It was definitely a positive thing.

But still, for a parent like me, being suddenly told that my daughter had cancer, abruptly separated from my husband and son for who knows how long, and living indefinitely in a hospital – well, I suppose I had nearly reached my limit. I doubt that I handled the process with good grace. I was really trying, but I am human, after all; a mother with a child who had a large, potentially cancerous tumor hiding in her body. I'm sure nurses and doctors are accustomed to parents behaving badly, and know how to handle them. Health care providers are blessed with strong wills and compassion to do what they do, and it is admirable.

Fortunately, the nurse seemed to understand my frustration, or perhaps she saw the fear in my eyes. She smiled sympathetically and asked if she could get me anything, and then left, closing the door behind her so that Mikayla and I could be alone with my aunt and friend.

After the Chemo Duck fiasco, we continued to wait. By 2:00 p.m., Mikayla was *very* tired and cranky. She was bored, hungry, and thirsty, and didn't understand why she couldn't even have a sip of water.

It was after 3:00 p.m. when they finally came for her. She was, of course, very scared. The crying began almost immediately and didn't stop. At her request, I carried her down to the surgery area, but she clung to me and cried the entire time.

They led us to a waiting room to administer a relaxant. Mikayla, exhausted and all cried out, fell asleep on my shoulder. I held her, rocking a little and stroking her hair and back. My aunt and friend waited with us, occasionally stroking *my* back or touching my shoulder, offering me wordless comfort as we waited. I was exhausted, but keyed up and on edge at the same time. My daughter was about to have a serious surgery. I was terrified. In the days following, I wouldn't be able to pick her up and squeeze her when she was afraid, because she'd have a long incision healing in addition to a very sore spot on her chest. Her low back would be bruised from the bone marrow biopsy.

A couple of nurses came and talked to us about anesthesia, and then they injected a relaxer that would also act as an amnesiac. They took Mikayla away from me after that and she whimpered groggily, holding her arms out and calling out one simple word over and over.

"Mommy!"

The moment Mikayla was out of sight, I lost it. I was holding her worn teddy bear, MoMo, who had accompanied us to the surgery area. The little polar bear smelled wonderfully familiar to me, just like my precious Mikayla. My aunt hugged me for a several moments, assuring me that Mikayla would not remember how she was taken away from me and brought into a strange room where several surgeons were waiting.

We had a few hours to pass now. My friend left and my aunt drove me to the Ronald McDonald House so I could shower. When we arrived, the House supervisor informed me that a larger room was available and I could move there if I wanted. This meant that there would be room for Kosta and Taki to stay with us whenever they flew down. I was relieved, remembering how Mikayla had cried that we had two twin beds instead of a bigger one that she could sleep with me in. We needed to move quickly though, since we had to get back to the hospital. Thank God for my aunt! I would not have been able to do everything on my own. While I showered, my aunt packed my things and cleaned the room per House regulations.

Halfway through the surgery, a nurse called to update us. They had completed the open biopsy, Mikayla's vitals were good, and they were about to do the other necessary procedures. My aunt and I quickly moved my things to the larger room and hurried back to the hospital. As we were walking back in, the nurse called again and told me that they were finished and the surgeon would meet me up in our room to discuss what had been done.

I paced the room anxiously for several very long minutes, my thoughts on Mikayla and the news we were about to hear. I wondered if I could handle what was coming.

The surgeon entered our room and spoke with my aunt and I before Mikayla was brought back. He explained a great deal about the tumor and the diagnosis possibilities, some of which I had not yet heard about. He brought the first bit of good news we had heard since the tumor had been discovered last week.

He explained that the tumor could be one of three things: neuroblastoma, ganglioneuroblastoma, or a ganglioneuroma.

The first possibility is the one that all the doctors thought the mass to be: neuroblastoma, the nerve cancer that would have to be staged and graded based on the biopsy results. If Mikayla had this, chemotherapy would be needed as well as a surgery at the end of treatment to remove the mass.

The second potential diagnosis was ganglioneuroblastoma. He explained that this was a tumor that is a cross between benign and malignant; certain parts of the mass were cancerous and would be treated with chemotherapy to rid the mass of the cancerous cells.

The last option confused me – a ganglioneuroma. This last diagnosis meant that a cell in Mikayla's body at birth or in utero began to form the neuroblastoma cancer. However, instead of remaining at the cancer stage and causing symptoms, the cell "self-destructs" somehow, and ends up as a benign tumor by the time the process is finished.

Benign tumor? I could hardly believe that possibility and still assumed that Mikayla had neuroblastoma. The doctors so far had all indicated that a tumor as large as Mikayla's was almost certainly cancer. In fact, almost every doctor we'd seen so far had specifically said they'd never seen a tumor like hers *not* have cancer in it.

As I struggled to understand what the surgeon was saying, he explained that a ganglioneuroma reaches full growth at some point and then stops growing, remaining in the body for life. Every tumor is different and there is no way to estimate what size the full growth will be. Ganglioneuromas often wrap themselves around the main arteries (such as in Mikayla's case) but do no harm, like a straw (the artery) going through a watermelon (the tumor). It just sits there; hence, no symptoms.

If Mikayla did have a ganglioneuroma, it would need to be monitored by her oncologist and surgeon back home to see if it continues to grow or has reached full growth already. If the tumor grew so much that it obstructed a major organ or began to squeeze the arteries it wrapped around, a surgery was necessary to remove it. However, surgery is not recommended if the tumor is not causing any symptoms. Chemotherapy cannot be used to shrink the tumor because there are no harmful cells for the therapy to target. Medical research indicates that ganglioneuroma tumors with this characterization never become neuroblastoma again, as the tumor cells were already cancerous and destroyed at some point.

The information was overwhelming and the doctor, seeing my strain, paused for a few moments to let it all absorb.

When he continued, he explained that during the biopsy, he extracted a piece of the tumor for a pathologist to examine. He decided to not put the Hickman catheter in Mikayla's chest since she may not have cancer and therefore would not need chemotherapy. If the diagnosis was cancer, another surgery would be needed to insert the Hickman catheter.

I was surprised by this. No line in the chest? That thing that Mikayla (and, to be honest, myself as well) was so afraid of wasn't there?

Not once since all the testing began had anyone thought the diagnosis could be non-cancerous, considering the tumor was already ten centimeters. It was too big and had already crossed the center line. We had arrived in Seattle fully expecting to begin chemotherapy treatments. The chance now that it may not be needed was astonishing and difficult to hope for.

The surgeon told us they would perform one more full-body scan in two days. That scan combined with the pathology result from the tumor's extracted piece would result in the final diagnosis.

It didn't seem possible to me that Mikayla might not have cancer. If the doctors thought it was a possibility, I would expect everyone to be throwing a party, or at least coming in with smiles and positive words. However, the doctors and nurses were still acting just as somber as they had been prior to the surgery. For a brief moment I even silently questioned the surgeon's credibility, considering that I didn't think good news was a possibility by now.

Fortunately, common sense overruled and I remembered that he knew what he was doing.

My aunt explained that the doctors had to be absolutely sure before making such a declaration. However, after discussing the options again, we both assumed that the surgeon was leaning more toward the diagnosis of ganglioneuroma because he had decided to not insert the Hickman catheter in Mikayla's chest. Now there was actually hope that Mikayla did not have cancer…

Shortly after the surgeon left, Mikayla was wheeled in. She was on a hospital bed, lying curled up on her side. She wore a little yellow hospital gown that had the cartoon characters Bugs Bunny, Tweety, Sylvester, and Taz on it. It seemed like she was asleep, but also slightly awake at the same time. She whimpered a little bit as they transferred her on to the bed in her room.

The nurse pulled up Mikayla's gown to show me the incision and my heart wrenched. Tears immediately stung my eyes as I saw a scar nearly three inches long which was a livid, dark red line surrounded by a yellowish-white patch of skin. There were two small purplish-red spots on her lower back, though her chest was thankfully unchanged. She was very pale and still had the IV attached as well. It hurt so much to see these marks on my daughter's body.

For the next couple of hours, my aunt and I talked over Mikayla as she slept. She would wince from time to time, automatically reaching a small hand to her side and letting out one piteous whimper of pain. Her eyes did not open at all.

I took a picture of her this way to show Kosta, and to forever remember. I hope that I will never again have to see one of our children in such a condition. Surgery is remarkable and often beneficial; however, I'd rather not have one of my children need it.

As the evening wound down, my aunt left and I was alone with my racing thoughts as I tried to sleep. I wondered yet again what could be going on inside my daughter's fragile body. Every moan she made that night alerted me, but it was always fleeting.

When a lab technician came in at 8:00 a.m. to draw blood, Mikayla did not even flinch. It was the first blood draw that had not been a traumatic experience, and the only one she never even realized had occurred.

CHAPTER NINE

~ Waiting ~

"Then ye shall call upon me, and ye shall go and pray unto me, and I will hearken unto you. And ye shall seek me, and find me, when ye shall search for me with all your heart."
~Jeremiah 29:12-13

October 30, 2008

Mikayla was given pain medication periodically throughout the night, and she continued sleeping when a doctor woke me to step outside and listen as he gave his report on Mikayla's condition. When I left the room, there was a group of ten or more medical personnel gathered around. This was a combination of oncologists, student doctors, and nurses. Mikayla's primary oncologist began to tell the others about Mikayla's vitals, her surgery experience, and the surgeon's decision to not insert the Hickman catheter.

Desperate for a bit of good news, I watched everyone very closely, trying to discern from their words or expressions whether or not they thought Mikayla might not have cancer. The lead oncologist stated to the others that the surgeon had not inserted the Hickman catheter in Mikayla's chest because they suspected ganglioneuroma.

I caught this particular phrasing and immediately interrupted.

"So, you *do* think that's what she has?!"

My anticipation of a non-cancer diagnosis immediately increased, and along with it came a sense of elation. However, several others hastened to tell me that there is no diagnosis one way or the other without the pathology report, and one of the head oncologists told me that she felt it was still neuroblastoma as she had seen many cases with a tumor just like Mikayla's in both size and characteristics, and never one that was not cancer. We would simply have to wait until the report came in.

When I returned to the room, Mikayla had just stirred. She smiled a little at me but was lethargic and did not move or talk much. Our friend from the previous day arrived to keep us company once again. He took one look at me – tired, worried, and stressed about the lack of diagnosis – and sent me off to get breakfast and call Kosta. He asked Mikayla if they could watch a movie together and she smiled. Her response was reassuring, so I left.

It was hard to eat, but I took my time, thinking about what the surgeon said and praying about the results. As any parent would, I desperately wanted a non-cancer diagnosis. I felt like I could hardly go on any further than what we had already endured, and knew that if the diagnosis came back as cancer that we still had a very long way to go. I called Kosta and we went through the possibilities again. It was difficult for him not being with us, and he was anxious to hear all that the doctors had said during their report.

When I returned to the room, they were watching Disney's *Tarzan* together. Mikayla barely noticed my entrance and remained engrossed in the movie until it was over. She asked if she could watch it again, which was amusing since she seemed ready to fall asleep. She was slightly groggy from the pain medication, but not as much as I had expected.

Mikayla slept much of the day and I anticipated five o'clock, when my mom was scheduled to arrive. Mikayla was excited by the prospect of seeing her grandma. Unfortunately, by this time, I had been running on too little sleep combined with too much stress, and I was beginning to feel sick. I was terrified at the thought that I could be developing a cold, because I knew if that were the case, the hospital staff would not allow me to stay. I dreaded the thought of leaving Mikayla for a few days while she recovered from surgery. I didn't know what to do.

Doctors and nurses came in and out all day, checking Mikayla's vitals and adjusting her pain medicine. Mikayla was cranky with the disturbances and ready to go home. By this time, she wasn't satisfied with the video chats. She wanted to see her daddy in person, not just on the computer. Every time they spoke now, she began to cry, "Daddy, I want to go *home*. I don't *want* to be in the hos-a-pul."

Fortunately, Mikayla did have two positive experiences. First, I was able to give her the news that the surgeon had not put the Hickman catheter in her chest. This brought out the hesitant reintroduction of Chemo Duck. He was not greeted with warm regard as most plush toys were, but Mikayla consented to look at him and smiled after she learned that she did not have that special tube in her chest like she thought she would. Perhaps Chemo Duck wasn't entirely bad after all.

The second bright moment came when my mom arrived. We hugged for a long time, which filled me with comfort and relief in that one simple action, as though I were transferring half of my burden to her in that moment. She brought Mikayla a gift, a little plush dachshund (a miniature of our real pet at home) in its own pink purse. Mikayla loved it and kept it next to her for the rest of the time she spent in the hospital. In fact, she happily agreed to exchange Chemo Duck for the dog. The new addition received a place of honor on her bed, second only to the beloved MoMo, and Chemo Duck disappeared once again.

After my mom arrived, two doctors came in to see us. I braced myself for bad news, expecting that malignant cells had been found in the tumor, but I was mistaken. The pathology report showed that the piece extracted from the tumor was benign!

The bit the surgeon had taken out was tiny, about one centimeter, so it was still possible that other parts of the tumor were cancerous. However, knowing that some of it was benign ruled out one diagnosis of the three – neuroblastoma, the most dreaded of them all. I was elated! At least the worst possibility had been ruled out. Instead of having a one-in-three chance of the diagnosis we hoped for, it was now an even fifty/fifty. I could hardly think and felt faint. My mom immediately instructed me to sit down to hear whatever else the doctors needed to say.

If any portions of the tumor were cancerous, the diagnosis would be ganglioneuroblastoma. Chemotherapy would target the cancerous cells and surgery would remove the tumor after chemotherapy treatments had been completed. If the tumor was entirely benign, Mikayla's diagnosis would be ganglioneuroma. A metaiodo-benzylguanidine scan (MIGB) would be done the next day. This is a nuclear scan test that would examine the cells' reaction to radioactive iodine. Any cells containing neuroblastoma would react in a specific way, confirming the presence of cancer.

My mom was optimistic although she tried not show it too much, knowing there was still a chance Mikayla might have some cancer cells in the tumor. She saw my stress level and knew I'd had little sleep. She insisted that I go back to the Ronald McDonald House that night and sleep, and assured me that she would stay with Mikayla that night. My fear of getting sick and being restricted from the ward outweighed my fear of being away from Mikayla for one night, so I finally agreed since Mikayla seemed okay with it.

My mom promised that she would call immediately if Mikayla needed me. It was odd to leave the hospital and go to my room at the House alone. It was the first time I'd been alone in a completely quiet, undisturbed place for days, and it felt strange. After spreading the news that neuroblastoma had been ruled out, I spent a lot of time in prayer and then slept heavily for hours.

October 31, 2008

I returned to the hospital by about 9:00 a.m. Mikayla had only been up long enough to have a nurse do her vitals, and she was very happy to see me. It was amazing how much more alert she seemed, considering that she was less than two days out of surgery. She was bored with her confinement and insisted on getting up and walking around, which she had not done yet. The IV was still connected and so she got up and walked from one side of the bed to the other, with me nervously following her. When I lifted her back into the bed, she wanted to get out again.

It was Halloween, and Mikayla was disappointed to be spending it in a hospital. Fortunately, the Child Life specialist showed up again with a gift – a Sleeping Beauty costume! She told us that there would be room-to-room trick-or-treating between two and four that afternoon. Unfortunately, Mikayla's MIBG scan was scheduled to occur right at that time. As it turned out, one of the hospital playrooms had a Halloween party going on. It was three floors below us and I couldn't think how it was possible to go with Mikayla barely thirty-six hours out of surgery. She had only walked a few steps and I thought she wouldn't be able to do much more than that, but the doctor said it would be okay if Mikayla really wanted to attend.

A Halloween party with costumes, games, and candy? Of course Mikayla wanted to go!

And so we went. We dressed Mikayla in her new Sleeping Beauty costume, pulling the sleeve carefully over her IV, and led her slowly out of the room. Mikayla wanted to wear the little heeled dress-up shoes that came with the outfit, but I put my foot down. I agreed to let her try them on and walk a couple steps, but that was it. She was disappointed, but I could imagine her tripping and falling on her tender abdomen and breaking the stitches.

We slowly made our way down to the party. I stayed with Mikayla, shielding her so she wouldn't get bumped, and my mom pushed the IV machine along behind her. Mikayla was excited and smiled continually, but I was very nervous. However, after several minutes, we made it to the party safely. There were a lot of people there, but most gave us a wide berth, smiling down at the cute little three-year-old Sleeping Beauty with the IV.

Mikayla received a large amount of

compliments, candies, and little prizes such as stickers and pencils. She tried throwing a bean bag through a hole and although she missed by several feet, she was rewarded with a stuffed animal. It is truly amazing what goes on in a children's hospital to make things special for the young patients. After half an hour, I told Mikayla we needed to go back to her room. We had to be ready for the upcoming scan.

When we returned to our room, Mikayla wanted to go back out in those heeled shoes. I agreed to let her take a short walk around the rooms while we waited for someone to come get us for the scan. A nurse came in a few minutes later and informed us that the scan was running behind schedule. This would normally have been frustrating, as Mikayla was fasting again and hungry, but this time it meant that we had a few extra minutes to participate in the room-to-room trick-or-treating. Mikayla loved it, slowly going from one room to the next as the nurses at each door gave her some candy. For me, the whole experience was strangely odd.

Every room we went to had a bed in it, of course, with a sick child. Some had no hair; some had tubes in their noses. But what really hit me the hardest was that several rooms had *cribs*. I had glimpsed hospital cribs when Mikayla was wheeled to the room after her first sedation. To see a crib actually set up with monitors in its own room was unsettling. A three-year-old child was, in my opinion, far too young to experience a life-threatening condition. But infants? I almost couldn't bear to look at those rooms. It hurt too much.

How many parents have watched their innocent babies fight for their lives with chemotherapy, rather than being able to watch and marvel at the first milestones such as sitting up, rolling over, or walking? My heart ached to know that many infants have spent most of their lives fighting for a chance to truly live. How precious is the life of *every* child, whether they take their first steps at home or in a hospital while connected to an IV.

The feeling of despondency stayed with me as we passed each room, and I wondered how many of the other children had the possibility of a non-cancer diagnosis. How many would be able to leave the hospital, healthy again at long last? How many more might lose the battle they fought so desperately?

After making a complete round of the ward and returning to our room with more candy than a three-year-old could ever manage to consume, it was finally time for the scan. This was a relief, as Mikayla was starving and only wanted to eat her candy. In the past four days, she had altogether eaten barely one meal. Mikayla has always been small, but she now looked more fragile and slight than she had two weeks ago. I hoped we would get a few days' break from the hospital to feed Mikayla a lot of food once the diagnosis was determined. With cancer treatment, Mikayla would have many more days where she would not be hungry.

We took Mikayla to the scanning room and anesthesia was used for the third time that week. I suppose it got easier to see her fade out suddenly when the anesthesia entered her body, but it was still not what I would call an *easy* experience for me as a parent. The scan itself was relatively quick and she was brought back to the room where my mom and I waited impatiently for the final verdict.

I was pacing the floor again, going back and forth from Mikayla's bed to the window. The doctors had already told us that they might not have new information for us until the next day or possibly Monday since it was Friday and the start of the weekend, but my mom thought they would be quicker if they could be, knowing that there was now a possibility of a non-cancer diagnosis.

She was right. Less than an hour later, two doctors entered our room, both bearing uncharacteristically wide smiles on their faces. They wasted no time on medical terminology or informative explanations, but immediately told me straight up – Mikayla had *no* sign of cancer *anywhere* in her body! The diagnosis was now officially a ganglioneuroma.

NO CANCER!

It was almost too good to believe.

God had given my precious little girl a miracle!

The feeling of relief – and disbelief – overwhelmed me so that I could hardly think above the pounding of my heart.

No cancer – none *at all*.

How on earth could a ten-centimeter abdominal mass lurking behind vital organs and wrapping around the body's main arteries not be cancerous? How could it actually, medically, be considered almost harmless? Was it even possible?

But then, with God, *all* things are possible. Even this.

CHAPTER TEN

~ Going Home ~

"Now unto him that is able to do exceeding abundantly above all that we ask or think, according to the power that worketh in us, unto him be glory in the church by Christ Jesus throughout all ages, world without end. Amen."
~Ephesians 3:20-21

Within two hours of the diagnosis, Mikayla received her discharge paperwork. During the entire time between the diagnosis and discharge, my mom and I took turns being on the phone to spread the news. Everything suddenly happened very quickly.

The two best things came first – telling Kosta, and telling Mikayla.

I could hardly even talk through the tears of joy when I spoke to my husband. I was so overcome that I could barely say the words, "She doesn't have cancer! We're coming *home*!"

We cried and laughed together, and spoke longingly of reuniting our family. In truth, it was only days that we were separated; however, it felt much longer than that, and had been filled with enough emotion to last a lifetime.

Kosta stayed on the phone while I told Mikayla the news. When I told her the miraculous diagnosis (referring back to the "bad apple" analogy – her bad apple was now just an apple), her eyes lit up. She was tired, hungry, and still a little groggy from the anesthesia, but she understood. She would get to see her daddy soon. She would be done with the hospital, with all the "shots and pokes and owies."

It took some time to pack up all the new toys and Halloween candy Mikayla had received while at the hospital. Our little stuffed Chemo Duck was unearthed again, but now he looked cute instead of threatening. Though ours to keep, Mikayla still didn't find him desirable enough to join the ranks of her plush buddies; my mom ended up with him instead.

He eventually was donated to our local hospital's chemotherapy ward.

The walk from the hospital room to the elevators was another odd mix of emotions for me – an experience I seemed to have quite frequently in the past days. I was smiling, of course, and rejoicing in my heart. But as we were leaving the hematology/oncology ward, I suddenly felt that it was unfair. As I walked away, I caught a glimpse of one of those crib beds again. I felt almost guilty to be leaving the ward with a non-cancer diagnosis, one of the very few I am sure they get. How is it that I was able to walk out with my daughter, when so many must stay?

I had a similar experience at the Ronald McDonald House.

Mikayla was not cleared to fly home until Monday, but we did not want to spend any minute longer than necessary in Seattle. Under other circumstances, I love visiting Seattle; but, after those few days, I was more than ready to leave and return at a different time when I actually planned a vacation instead of a hospital stay for a member of my family. When we returned to the House and relayed the news of Mikayla's diagnosis, they offered us the room through the weekend, but my mom and I agreed that it was time to leave. Knowing that there was a waiting list for families needing rooms, we felt we should not stay.

My mom had many family members that lived only a couple hours away by drive, so we decided to visit them until we could fly home. Mikayla would be able to see her great-grandparents, aunts, uncles, and cousins, who had been praying for her and planning to visit us in the hospital during the next week since we had thought she would still be undergoing tests or beginning cancer treatment.

However, while we were in the hallway near our room, we saw another family who was staying in a room across from ours. There was a father and mother, both probably in their early thirties, and two small children. The oldest was a boy just over two years old – the same age as my own son. The younger child was a ten-month-old girl.

After talking for a moment, we learned that the family had been at the House for five months while their infant daughter went through chemotherapy. At five months of age, she had been diagnosed with neuroblastoma, the very same cancer Mikayla had been thought to have. After five months of treatment – fully half of this little girl's life! – she was declared cancer-free and ready to go home.

I immediately had that overwhelming ache in my heart again. These parents had endured so much more than I had, and my path could have been the same. These two little girls with an adrenal mass in common – how precious their lives are. I still think of that baby girl from time to time, and hope that she has remained cancer-free.

After we left the House, I was amazed at how quickly Mikayla recovered during the next few days. She hardly complained of pain in her incision at all. A medicine as simple as Tylenol was all she needed.

It is remarkable how those little bodies can knit themselves together so quickly. We enjoyed the weekend among family, who celebrated with us and prayed for Mikayla's continued health and quick recovery. Even among family, though, we longed to return home. Monday finally arrived.

Mikayla again enjoyed all the aspects that surround a plane ride, though perhaps less than the previous trip, given that she was anxious to see her daddy again. My heart was racing with excitement when we landed, and I could see my own joy reflected in my daughter's face as well. Home again! Thank you, God!

I will never forget the moment in the airport when my precious family was reunited. We were at the baggage claim waiting as I frequently glanced over my shoulder to search for my husband. After a few minutes, I saw him, carrying my sweet little son, whose face lit up like a star when he caught sight of us. Kosta put him down and Taki ran toward me as fast as his little two-year-old legs could carry him.

"Mama! Mama!"

Could there be anything better to me than this moment, with my son cuddled so close? I doubt it. Except perhaps what I saw when I turned around – my daughter with her arms around her daddy, head on his shoulder, while he held her as though she was the most precious, fragile doll. There were tears in his eyes, and a smile on his face.

By the grace of God, we were home again. Cancer-free.

EPILOGUE

~ Continuation ~

"For in thee, O Lord, do I hope: thou wilt hear, O Lord my God."
~Psalm 38:15

My beautiful little girl, our only daughter, is six years old now. Our precious son is five, and we also have a one-year-old son as a sweet addition to our lives. God has blessed us with a beautiful family, and three children that are healthy. Health is indeed a thing to be cherished, but instead is too often undervalued. Perhaps I had always taken for granted that my children were "normal" and healthy. I will never do so again. Every time I look at my daughter, I remember.

If there is anything we have learned from our

walk through the valley, it is the blessing that life is. Hold your loved ones longer; hug them at every chance you get; teach them kindness and love, and to regard others with respect and compassion. Don't forget to take time to play together or read them their favorite stories. Childhood will not last forever.

I do not presume to understand the pain of losing a child to death, nor do I know what it is like to experience cancer in a child and spend months or even years battling it. My own journey through the valley was but a small taste of what many others have endured. While we rejoice at the diagnosis our daughter received, my heart aches for those who have gone through far more than we did.

The time spent in silent prayer during that awful ordeal was uncountable. I only know that minute by minute, day by day, God himself walked me through. I truly could not see ahead to the next day, and knew that I could only focus on getting through one single day at a time. Even amid the heartbreak and trauma, I felt the peace of God pressing upon me, urging me forward. He loves my daughter with an everlasting love, a love that I could not even begin to understand. He loves me in the same way, as he does each and every one of his children. Such a gift is priceless.

The endless prayers and support we received from our family and friends was incredible. Such an outpouring of love over us was a blessing. We were lifted up in prayer across the United States and even overseas. The love for one another, under God, is truly an amazing thing. As it is written in the Bible:

> *"For where two or three are gathered together in my name, there am I in the midst of them."*
> *~Matthew 18:20*

The nature of Mikayla's tumor is uncommon. Most tumors of its size and location would be cancerous. The miracle we were blessed with is that it is *not*. Though the large tumor wrapped around arteries remains a matter of concern, we no longer fear that our daughter has, or will develop, cancer.

Based on research, the doctors believe that the cancer cells have already been destroyed; that threat has passed.

At the time of the diagnosis, we were told that a ganglioneuroma will eventually reach full growth and could remain in her body for life, causing no problems. We just do not know what that full growth size is.

Mikayla requires regular check-ups to observe any growth or change in the tumor's characteristics. She is so young that we do not have any idea if the full growth has been reached. After returning home from Seattle, the tumor remained unchanged for a year and a half, though we don't know how long it took to expand to ten centimeters as it was when we first discovered it.

In June of 2010, a scan showed a sudden increase in size and volume by twenty-five percent. Her tumor had expanded from ten to about thirteen centimeters at some point in the six months between scans. This growth alarmed us and she was closely watched, with another scan performed three months later. At that time, and again in March of 2011, the tumor was unchanged and remained at thirteen centimeters.

Though Kosta and I were uncomfortable with this sudden growth, the doctors were not unduly alarmed. Since the tumor wraps around major arteries, they believe that the tumor itself will, from time to time, grow and change as Mikayla does to accommodate her body's development. The doctors monitor Mikayla's blood pressure, among other things, to ensure that all is well with the flow of blood through these arteries and the liver.

Though it is not expected, and Mikayla's case is now considered long-term care since there is no cancer, there is always the chance that the tumor could begin to affect her body by obstructing other organs or squeezing too tightly on the arteries. Should that happen, her doctors are now confident that they could remove the tumor completely in a surgery that would take about sixteen hours. They would remove it bit by bit, scraping it carefully off of the arteries it clings to.

As parents, we hope that the tumor never requires this, since the surgery itself can be a great risk. I can hardly imagine seeing Mikayla go through surgery again, especially at an age now where she would understand more, remember more, and possibly fear more. At other times, we wish we could get it over with and rid her body completely of the tumor. We will continue to closely monitor her, to ensure that any changes that come will not harm her body. In September of 2011, an ultrasound showed another change – this time, the tumor shrank to about nine centimeters, a volume decrease of thirty percent. It could continue to shrink or expand again, which is why the follow-ups are important.

Either way, God is in control. He knew what was happening in Mikayla's body long before we ever did, and we know that he loves her far more than we could ever comprehend. He was by our side continually as we walked through the valley, and he brought us safely through the experience. Even if the outcome had been different, we know God would still have remained by our side through it all. The consistent check-ups serve as a reminder to us of the precious life each and every person is blessed with.

We pray for Mikayla continually, that her body will remain unaffected by tumor. She has grown to be a very compassionate person through this experience, and is especially aware of children with cancer. She occasionally donates her money to cancer causes, gives toys and books to kids that are in the hospital for cancer treatment, and participates in fundraisers to benefit cancer research. We are blessed to witness her giving heart and tender compassion for others.

Savor each day – it is a blessing God has given you.

NOTE FROM THE AUTHOR

Sadly, there are many kinds of childhood cancers. Neuroblastoma develops in several hundred new cases per year, and is most common in infants and young children. To my knowledge, it is the only type of cancer that can actually "self-destruct" and return to a benign state, as it did in my own daughter; however, this is a less common occurrence.

St. Jude Children's Research Hospital, founded in 1962, is an active organization in the research and treatment of children's cancer today. You can learn more facts about childhood cancers and about St. Jude's vision at *www.stjude.org*.

The Ronald McDonald House Charities maintains homes designed to house the families of and patients with childhood cancers. Patients and families may come and stay as long as they need to. There are houses spread across the Unites States of America, and even in other countries. You can learn more about Ronald McDonald House Charities at *www.rmhc.org*.

9613837R0010

Made in the USA
Charleston, SC
27 September 2011